Sleaze

Ed Adams

a firstelement production

Ed Adams

First published in Great Britain in 2022 by firstelement
Copyright © 2022 Ed Adams
Directed by thesixtwenty

10 9 8 7 6 5 4 3 2

A CIP catalogue record for this book is available from the British
Library.

ISBN 13: 978-1-913818-22-7

eBook ISBN: 978-1-913818-23-4

Printed and bound in Great Britain by Ingram Spark

rashbre
an imprint of firstelement.co.uk
rashbre@mac.com

ed-adams.net

Live the questions now.

Rainer Maria Rilke

Thanks

A big thank you for the tolerance and bemused support from all of those around me. To those who know when it is time to say, " step away from the keyboard!" and to those who don't.

To Julie for an understanding that only comes with really knowing.

To thesixtwenty.co.uk for direction.

To the NaNoWriMo gang for the continued inspiration and encouragement.

To Topsham, for being lovely.

To the edge-walkers. They know who they are.

And, of course, thanks to the extensive support via the random scribbles of rashbre via
http://rashbre2.blogspot.com
and its cast of amazing and varied readers whether human, twittery, smoky, artistic, cool kats, photographic, dramatic, musical, anagrammed, globalized or maxed.

Not forgetting the cast of characters involved in producing this; they all have virtual lives of their own.

And of course, to you, dear reader, for at least 'giving it a go'.

Books by Ed Adams include:

Triangle Trilogy		About
1	The Triangle	Dirty money? Here's how to clean it
2	The Square	Weapons of Mass Destruction – don't let them get on your nerves
3	The Circle	The desert is no place to get lost
4	The Ox Stunner	The Triangle Trilogy – thick enough to stun an ox
		(all feature Jake, Bigsy, Clare, Chuck Manners)
Archangel Collection		
1	Archangel	Sometimes I am necessary
2	Raven	An eye that sees all between darkness and light
3	Card Game	Throwing oil on a troubled market
4	Magazine Clip	the above three in one heavy book.
5	Play On, Christina Nott	Christina Nott, on Tour for the FSB
6	Corrupt	Trouble at the House
7	Sleaze	Autos, Politics, Gstaad
		(all feature Jake, Bigsy, Clare, Chuck Manners)
Big Science Textbook		
1	Coin	Get rich quick with Cybercash – just don't tell GCHQ
2	An Unstable System	Creating the right kind of mind
3	The Watcher	We don't need no personal saviours here
4	Jump	Some kind of future
5	Pulse	Want more? Just stay away from the edge
Blade's Edge Trilogy		
1	Edge	World end climate collapse and sham discovered during magnetite mining from Jupiter's moon Ganymede.
2	Edge Blue	Earth's endgame, unless…
3	Edge Red	An artificially intelligent outcome, unless…
4	Edge of Forever	Edge Trilogy

About Ed Adams Novels:

Triangle Trilogy		About
1	Triangle	Money laundering
2	Square	A viral nerve agent being shipped by terrorists and WMDs
3	Circle	In the Arizona deserts, with the Navajo; about missiles stolen from storage.
4	Ox Stunner	the above three in one heavy book.
		(all feature Jake, Bigsy, Clare, Chuck Manners)
Archangel Collection		
1	Archangel	Biographical adventures of Russian trained Archangel, who, as Christina Nott, threads her way through other Triangle novels.
2	Raven	Big business gone bad and being a freemason won't absolve you
3	Card Game	Raven Pt 2 – Russian oligarchs attempt to take control
4	Magazine Clip	the above three in one heavy book.
5	Play On, Christina Nott	Christina Nott, on Tour for the FSB
6	Corrupt	Parliamentary corruption
7	Sleaze	Autos, Politics, Gstaad
		(all feature Christina Nott, Jake, Bigsy, Clare, Chuck Manners)
Big Science Textbook		
1	Coin	Cyber cash manipulation by the Russian state.
2	An Unstable System	Creating the right kind of mind
3	Jump	Some kind of future
4	The Watcher	From the Big Bang to the almost Almighty Whimper
5	Pulse	Sci-Fi dystopian blood management with nano-bots
Blade's Edge Trilogy		
1	Edge	World end climate collapse and sham discovered during magnetite mining from Jupiter's moon Ganymede.
2	Edge Blue	Endgame, for Earth – unless?
3	Edge Red	Museum Earth – unless?
4	Edge of Forever	Edge Trilogy

Ed Adams Novels: Links

Triangle Trilogy		Link:	Read?
1	Triangle	https://amzn.to/3c6zRMu	
2	Square	https://amzn.to/3sEiKYx	
3	Circle	https://amzn.to/3qLavYZ	
4	Ox Stunner	https://amzn.to/3sHxlgh	
Archangel Collection			
1	Archangel	https://amzn.to/2Y9nB5K	
2	Raven	https://amzn.to/2MiGVe6	
3	Raven's Card	https://amzn.to/2Y8HLgs	
4	Magazine Clip	https://amzn.to/3pbBJYn	
5	Play On, Christina Nott	https://amzn.to/2MbkuHl	
6	Corrupt	https://amzn.to/2M0HnOw	
7	Sleaze	https://amzn.to/3sE3UDt	
8	An Unstable System	https://amzn.to/2PRJciF	
Big Science Textbook			
1	Coin	https://amzn.to/3o82wmS	
2	An Unstable System	https://amzn.to/2PRJciF	
3	Jump	https://amzn.to/3kTFWjg	
4	The Watcher	https://amzn.to/3sCzK3h	
5	Pulse	https://amzn.to/3qQlBvL	
Edge of forever Trilogy			
1	Edge	https://amzn.to/2KDmYOW	
2	Edge Blue	https://amzn.to/2Kyq9au	
3	Edge Red	https://amzn.to/2KzJwjz	
4	Edge of Forever	https://amzn.to/3c57Ghj	

Thanks   **4**
    Books by Ed Adams include: 5
    About Ed Adams Novels: 6
    Ed Adams Novels: Links   7

PART ONE   **12**

Singapore   **13**
    Fringe benefits   14
    Caffè Concerto   18
    Fleet's In   21
    Cold beer and delivery pizza   31
    Back, once again   35

I'm in love with my car   **43**
    Triangle office   44
    Lady driver   50
    Above the fold   52
    Amanda calls   55
    Tony Brooklands   58
    Road to Zero   68

Jockey full o' bourbon   **72**
    Whiskey Sour   73
    Aberdeen Pop up chargers   76
    Travel brochures   82
    Another Table   85
    A visit to Lottie   88
    Xmas Party   90
    Wolseley   96
    Back to Bermondsey   100
    Cat returns with information   107

Right through you   **109**
    Undetectable Firearms Act   110

Kotyonok   131
Geneva   134
Breakfast   140
Rinse and repeat every breakfast   145
Range anxiety   149
The Raft   158
Firework Nirvana   162
Breakfast with dark glasses   171
Reconfigurable Electric Drive Matrix (REDM)   176
Bérénice Charbonnier   198
Cars to Gstaad   203

PART TWO   **206**

Toblerone   **208**
About Gstaad   209
The right to disconnect   215
Helipad   218
Zopf   226
Studded tyres   229
It's the glacier talking!   231
Monday at the Gstaad expo   237
A two-stage thing   247
Gangsta rap   253
Carrots and sticks   257
Pressure Point   262
Hannah's disappearance   264
Second Order thinking   271
Small airstrip, big helicopter   274
Suspicion-less   276
Window dressing   285
Intense   288
Brading's Office   290
Portcullis House   298

China, my China   **311**

China   312
Deflect, Distract, and Brazen it out   322
Committee Room   331
Recording   336

PART THREE   **338**

lived in bars   **339**
Partition revealed   340
What we've found   343
Breaking up with a drunkard   348
Cafe Churchill   350
Clare's article   354
Floundering   359
Safe to cross streets   361
Badge engineering   365
Advice   369
Process, not Event   371
Unbelievable   378
You're Undetectable   379
Infrastructure Improvement Committee Session   383
Fireworks   390

China   **394**
700 per cent   395
Generous donors   398
Free-for-all?   405
Wrap up   417

PART ONE

Singapore

We sail tonight for Singapore
We're all as mad as hatters here
I've fallen for a tawny moor
Took off to the land of nod

Drank with all the china men
Walked the sewers of Paris
I danced along a coloured wind
Dangled from a rope of sand
You must say goodbye to me

We sail tonight for Singapore
Take your blankets from the floor
Wash your mouth out by the door
The whole town's made of iron ore
Every witness turns to steam
They all become Italian dreams

Fill your pockets up with earth
Get yourself a dollar's worth
Away boys, away boys, heave away
The captain is a one-armed dwarf
He's throwing dice along the wharf
In the land of the blind
The one-eyed man is king, so take this ring

Tom Waits

Fringe benefits

"Clare, we'll miss you and your fringe benefits!" said Tessa. She looked dreamily at the first remover and he winked, "Any chance of a cup of tea?"

Two lads with a white van were assisting Clare Crafts leave Bermondsey and her researcher life in Parliament. Lottie Trevethick and Tessa Maier, her two flat-shares, were sad to see Clare go, but perked up as soon as they saw the two fit-looking young men emerge from the van.

The first remover sounded well-spoken and Lottie asked him, "So, is this your main job?"

"No, Hugo over there runs a hot air ballooning business and I'm an actor. My name is Bjorn, and so you can probably guess that my mother is Swedish." He didn't have a trace of accent and sounded as if he was from west London.

"Have I seen you in anything?" asked Lottie, and Bjorn answered, "Only 'Prime Suspect', but it didn't end well for me. Apart from that, I do some stage acting to keep the wolf from the door. Oh, and this man-in-a-van stuff, too. And some contract gardening."

Clare smiled. It was turning into another typical day in the life of the flat and she wondered if she would miss it. Then her phone rang. 'Rachel Crosby' it said on the screen. Rachel was a lobby journalist for The Post - someone whom Clare had met on her very first day as a Researcher in Parliament, and even been warned not to trust. But since those early days, Clare and Rachel had worked out that they worked better together than in opposition.

"Rachel! An unexpected surprise!"

"Hello Clare. A little birdy told me that you were moving on now the business with the manipulated politicians has passed?"

"They are literally moving my stuff out of Bermondsey as we speak!"

"Well, I think I may have something for you. Assuming you are still interested in cases of extreme corruption?"

"It can't be on such an industrial scale as the last situation," answered Clare.

"No, agreed, but this one has a way to make vast amounts of cash through the chumocracy," answered Rachel, "I've received some tipoffs. It'd mean more work inside Parliament."

Clare had originally been asked to work in Parliament clandestinely, to support Amanda Miller, who was a special services long-term acquaintance of Clare and the others who made up an informal working arrangement known as The Triangle.

Working with Rachel was an altogether different thing. Clare was aware that Rachel was an investigative journalist and that this could go in any number of directions.

Previously, Clare with Jake, Bigsy and Christina had uncovered systemic corruption of the lobby system in Parliament through what would best be described as moral suasion (also known as blackmail). It had proved to be a very cost-effective way to get lobbyists into position and to influence the direction of government.

Once the whole situation had been closed with the involvement of SI6 and other agencies, Clare had agonised over whether to move away from Parliament, or whether to continue providing support to her MP Andrew Brading. Brading was now the Secretary of State for Internal Affairs, a senior governmental position.

Clare paused for a moment, then replied, "Well I guess we'd better meet!"

"How about Caffè Concerto, in Whitehall?" asked

Rachel.

Clare knew it as an informal Italian cafe and, whilst on Whitehall, it was also somewhere to escape from the usual Parliament set.

"Great!" answered Clare and arranged a time for their meeting. She would bring someone else along. Someone from the Triangle.

"Always in demand!" said Lottie, noting that Clare had finished the call.

"They may want me to do something else," answered Clare, "Still with Parliament!"

"Oh. Do stay on!" exhorted Lottie, "Even if you want to live in your fancy west-London apartment!"

Caffè Concerto

Caffè Concerto

Clare knew the Caffè Concerto well. It was the one a short distance from Trafalgar Square and nestled between a small library-style pub and a MacDonald's.

Inside the Caffè was mirrored glitter and sparkling chandeliers. The friendly waiter approached and showed Clare and her accomplice Jake to a table. One side was a long banquette seat, so it would be possible to squish many people in when the need arose. At this quiet time, the venue was almost deserted. Rachel arrived within a minute and they all sat around a small table for four.

"Hello Rachel, you already know Jake, don't you?"

They all stood and greeted one another with hugs.

"Yes, when that business with the Medusa Station was unfolding,"

Jake spoke, "Hi Rachel, this sounds intriguing, but I'm wondering whether you are going to need some further support, based upon what happened in that other incident."

"You know, I was hoping you would say that. I'll tell you what I know, but I am concerned that I've got in somewhat deep."

Jake and Clare looked at Rachel. She was normally calm and collected, but this time looked a little unsettled.

Jake spoke again, "Ground rules first, no hidden recording devices, please."

"You have my word, " answered Rachel, "And you also?"

They all laughed.

A waited came across and took an order. They skirted around the Luxury Afternoon Tea and settled for a coffee and a cake each.

"Prosecco as well?" asked the waiter hopefully, but they all shook their heads.

Rachel began, "You'll have seen some articles in the news about Pay to Play lobbying and Cash for Questions. It's even more convoluted than the press has so far discovered. And your old friends Brant are involved."

"I don't think we'll ever get away from them," said Clare.

Jake nodded, "Brant and Raven Holdings and I think they have set up another subsidiary called Biotree now, as well."

Fleet's In

Rachel explains

"It stated when I visited Douglas Lessiter, MP at his home. Remember he is also a slightly improbable Minister of State for Infrastructure. It was his idea actually and I met him with his researcher Hannah. You must know Hannah - she looks like Nicole Kidman?"

"Yes, I met her during my first day, and we've become friends over my time in Parliament. She has helped me navigate some of the tricksier situations. Oh, as well as Lottie and Tessa, of course. And if Lessiter is a Minister of State, he's a level below Andrew Brading?"

"Yes, that is correct - although he can still attend Cabinet Meetings and his single function title is somehow more powerful than the top jobs with titles like: Secretary of State for Levelling Up, Housing and Communities; Minister for Intergovernmental Relations. If you know what I mean."

Rachel pauses and then says, "Well, I'll come clean. I was looking around for any sort of story from after that Andrew Brading faux-pas when he got caught in that mis-quote about Black Lives Matter. I seem to remember that you, Clare, fixed it with a couple of sound bites. Nicely done, and it diverted attention away so quickly. Then that pizza story broke and everyone was on to the next thing."

"Oh yes the 24-hour news cycle," mutters Jake.

"Well, I was interested to know if Andrew Brading and Clare were working in tandem and that it was some kind of stunt pulled by Serena McMillan - Andrew's office manager and that other researcher Maggie Shannon. I wondered if the whole thing was somehow staged to take attention from another story."

"I see," says Clare, "That's why you went to Duggie? Because he's the MP next door in Westminster. You wanted to find out whether Duggie or even Hannah knew anything?"

"I always knew you were cute," says Rachel, "You are exactly right."

Clare notices Jake nodding at Rachel's admission.

He says, "You remind me of my time working for the ladmag 'Street', which was always looking for after-dirt on any celeb stories. I guess you are doing the same thing for politicos."

Rachel smiles, "I didn't know you'd worked for Street! I had an ex who worked for them - Rafe Chesterton? Maybe you knew him?"

"Oh yes, we all knew Rafe - he was one of the founders of the magazine - We used to laugh about the way he pretended to be a gangster, until we realised, he really was one.

Rachel smirks, "Yes and Street was only one of his publications, all of which were very close to the gutter. Oh, sorry, no offence meant. I first met this apparently lavish and chivalrous man, but soon realised he was a two-timing liar frequently operating on the wrong side of the law. It didn't stop him from amassing money though. Now he's got a property investment company which leases High Street stores and I think he's got something to do with a Premier League team."

"Maybe it's a handy laundromat for him?" snickers Jake.

Rachel continues, "Yes, well back to Douglas Lessiter. He poured out the wine and attempted to answer my questions. I think I learned more about him than I did about anything to do with Brading during that session. Hannah was dutifully supporting him, but I could see that she'd been made to come along. I think Lessiter was aiming for an impression of some sort of frisson between them, but I could see it was all a sham. I mean, he had a Paul Cadmus on the wall - 'Fleets In', with the

French bread-sticks and men on bicycles."

Jake shakes his head, "No I don't know that piece,"

"It's a piece of iconic symbolism of a particular kind," explains Rachel, through raised eyebrows.

"Oh - I see! Likes men! The penny has dropped," splutters Jake through his pastry.

Rachel and Clare both laugh.

"Well in addition to his self-image polishing, Lessiter also mentioned something else. That there was still a type of politician who could get very rich by adjusting the terms of their service. Not only that, but there were also several support structures to help them conceal what they were doing."

"But does this have anything to do with the old situation that we uncovered?" asks Clare.

"No, Lessiter was very clear that this seemed to originate from within Westminster and was mainly of interest to those in higher positions. He said it seemed to be we'll-funded and could be ruthless with people who stood in its path. I watched Hannah's reaction to the story, and I had the distinct impression that she was hearing it for the very first time. Lessiter didn't think Brading was involved or even aware of it. And both held the opinion that Brading was as straight as a die."

Rachel continues, "I just have a chance to look

around the room when Hannah says they are pushed for time. She's rumbled that I was looking for something about Brading, not Lessiter. I get the impression that she thinks Lessiter said too much about the illicit operation in Westminster. I notice that there's an obvious workstation at one side of the living area with two huge computer screens. I realise it must be Hannah's and then I realise that she must be a live-in assistant."

Rachel continues, "The living space is divided from the kitchen by a dining table. There's another computer, a laptop this time, and a stack of cardboard folders, several of which were opened as if research was in progress. I noticed that the word 'Silverstone' seemed prominent, like it was the name of the file collection."

"Silverstone - car racing," says Jake," and traffic jams."

"I did the 'glance at watch' thing, 'I guess that's our time over, thank you for the hospitality.' Lessiter stands up, smoothes his tie. He looks as if he's sorry to see me go."

"Then he said it: 'Have you heard the latest stupid rumour about me?' Hannah caught my eye over Lessiter's shoulder. A sympathetic if slightly pained twitch of her mouth. I watched as she tucks her blonde hair behind her ear with a free hand, then reaches for a fresh glass of wine like a woman who really needs a drink. Lessiter continues, 'One of the red tops, is gunning for me now. Innuendo, but the third day of it. I was hoping...' Then his voice trailed off. I thought he should change his decor at least and maybe get a photoshoot to promote his all-new alpha image."

Rachel continues, " 'Look, I'm not sure how I can help you,' I said, all the time thinking that he had given me some potentially big news, not about Brading, but about a whole system of sleaze operating within the corridors of power."

"So that's when you left?" asks Jake, "I'd call it a result. You got a whole new story, plus hints of the Lessiter situation."

"Yes, but I'd need a photographer along for the Lessiter segment. 'Hottie dates MP' etc. That'd do it."

Jake laughs, and Clare notices several people in the Caffè look toward him.

"We're creating a small scene in here," Clare hisses, and looks carefully around to ensure there were no faces from Parliament around.

"Okay, well, I thought you'd like to know that the situation you ended is still dead, but a replacement scam has been initiated by some of Parliament's actual participants. We could work together on this?"

Then, from Rachel, a short nod. She looks away, starts to wrap her hair around her fingers, twisting and unravelling it as she talks. "This isn't just about me. It's about my brother. David. Dr David Crosby. He was a computer scientist who founded and ran a UK/Israeli data security start-up in Liverpool. They had a big contract with the UK Government. Something to do with message filtering." Clare notices Rachel's use of past tense.

"He killed himself just over a year ago."

"Oh, I'm so sorry," says Jake, "Can you talk about it?" He looks concerned and Clare realises she was watching two professional news gatherers both on their best game.

Rachel replies, "I don't, actually. You are now part of a handful of people who I've told - outside family, of course."

"So, what happened?" asks Clare, gently.

"No-one really knows. He drove to the coast and drowned himself. Wallasey. His body wasn't even in the sea. He was in a Marine Pool at Wallasey. His car was neatly parked but there wasn't even CCTV coverage of him arriving in the area.

"Wallasey? That's near Birkenhead?" asks Jake.

"Yes, in the Wirral, right where the Mersey turns into open sea."

"They wanted his body to be found, then?" says Jake.

"They?" queries Rachel.

"We'll, I'm guessing an open verdict," says Jake.

Clare notices water in Rachel's eyes.

"Jake, stop," she says.

Rachel turns to them both. She gently wipes away tears, "We journalists are a suspicious lot. I couldn't believe David would have just fallen into the water, which is what the coroner said."

She continues, "I received an email from him before I even knew he'd died. It said his security system had noticed some unusual messaging traffic from around Parliament. He suspected there was something untoward happening. He even attached a file, which was a log - all in computer-speak."

"Did you look into it?" asks Jake.

"I did at the time. No-one could work it out and I didn't want it to become a big thing, where I started to become the story. You, Jake, know how it is. My experts told me that the log seemed to imply that someone was setting up a new kind of lobbying operation,"

"Medusa mark III?" asks Jake, "Not again!"

"Well - At the time I linked the two events together. David's computer discovery and Lessiter's implication that there was well-funded clandestine lobbying operation at Westminster."

"Or is it just what you want to believe?" asks Jake.

"I wondered that too, but I didn't tell the experts looking at the computer logs anything about what Lessiter had told me."

Clare grimaces, "Hmm, but let's face it, Lessiter is not the most discreet of individuals."

"Agreed, but Lessiter seemed to be telling this story for the first time. I could tell that Hannah had not heard it before."

Rachel pauses, then continues. "The thing is it is very similar to what my brother had discovered. It makes me think that cutting one head from the serpent only reveals another one hiding behind."

"Rachel, can we think about this, please? I'll be able to give you an answer but it could take me a couple of days."

"Sure, that's fine. I've sat on this for a long time already. Knowing you were about to leave Parliament gave me a catalyst to act."

Clare smiles back at Rachel.

"I just wish we'd been able to be this frank sooner."

"I know, it's amazing the difference when someone isn't directly connected with the Westminster Bubble."

Clare looks at Jake, as if to say, 'time's up.' Jake gets the message and stands.

"Look, Rachel, it has been very pleasant to meet you today and I think you've put some interesting ideas in front of us both. I'm certain we'd have ways we could help, but you can understand that Clare needs time. After all, she was planning to leave Parliamentary duties today."

Rachel also stands. Clare and Jake can see her look of pleading for help, although she is too professional to ask for help directly.

"Okay, we'll see how this works out over the next few days. May I call you, in say three days?" she asks Clare.

"That's fine Rachel, I'll look forward to our conversation. Jake settles the bill and the three of them leave the Caffè, Rachel almost immediately hiring a cab for a fast get-away.

"You' coming around, and I'll call Bigsy so that we can talk?" suggests Jake.

Clare nods, "Good plan."

Cold beer and delivery pizza

By the time they reach Jake's, Bigsy is already there. He is sitting on the doorstep and stands as they approach.

"I thought you had a key?" asks Jake.

"I do, but I wasn't sure you'd remember," replies Bigsy, "Anyhow, I've only been here for a few minutes."

Jake opens the door and the three of them step into Jake's flat. Ground floor, with a large living room at the front, and a smaller kitchen and dining room at the back. Wooden table, metal fittings, industrial chic. A big industrial clock on the wall behind their heads

Without ceremony, they seat themselves around the dining table. Jake pulls three cold beers from the fridge.

"Okay, so what have you two been up to?" asks Bigsy.

"We met with Rachel Crosby today. It was Clare's last day in the apartment."

"Oh, yes, I'd semi-forgotten. How did it go?" asked Bigsy.

"Fine, in terms of the move, less so in terms of the overall outcome," answered Clare.

"There's good reason for Clare to stay on longer," explains Jake.

They recount their meeting with Rachel to Bigsy.

Then, as they finish, there is a pause.

Bigsy breaks the silence, "It looks like you'll be staying on in Westminster for a while, Clare."

Jake nods and Clare gives a palpable sigh of relief. "Oh, that's great - I wondered if you thought I was mad to do this?"

"No, I guess we owe Rachel one for her help with the Medusa thing, and it also sounds as if she has some unresolved issues of her own linked with all of this," answered Bigsy.

"We'd better inform Christina too," says Jake, "She'll be back from Amsterdam tomorrow afternoon."

Clare looks at both Jake and Bigsy.

"We're forgetting one fundamental thing. I no longer have access to Parliament. My green badge and contracts all finished today."

"But has Andrew Brading already hired your replacement?" asks Bigsy, "Couldn't you say you'd prefer to stay on?"

"I guess that would be Serena's decision - she's the office manager, " answers Clare.

"Right - you must have her mobile number?" asks Jake, "Call her now, before events overtake us."

Clare stands, "I'm going into your living room. I hope that's okay?" she looks at Jake.

Jake nods, "What will you say?"

"I'll simply ask for my old job back!"

Clare walks out of the kitchen, along a short hallway and into the living room.

Bigsy looks at Jake.

"She's so well thought of, they'll be delighted," says Jake.

Ten minutes later, Jake had found three more bottles of beer, and Bigsy had ordered delivery pizza.

Clare reappears. She is smiling. "Job done! I'm back in business. Serena was quite excited. She was going to tell Andrew Brading and Maggie Shannon tonight. I'd better check my phone is charged!"

"Best to call Rachel next," says Jake.

"What about your flatmates?" asks Bigsy, "Won't Lottie and Tessa think it a little strange when they see you in Parliament again?"

"They were next on my list. At least I've been able to tell them about my Apartment in Chelsea and they won't be at all surprised at my sudden change of direction!"

Jake walks back to the fridge. This time he returns with a bottle of Bollinger Brut and some pre-chilled champagne flutes.

"Ahah!" says Bigsy, "Good enough for Double-0-Seven, good enough for our clandestine operator!"

"Cheers, everyone," says Jake, "And congratulations to Clare on the start of another adventure!"

They clink glasses.

"Okay if I use your living room for a while to make some more phone calls?" asks Clare.

Back, once again

The next day, Clare had some of the feelings that she'd had on her very first day in Parliament. She'd called up Samantha, her sister, and explained about leaving and then not.

"Why am I not surprised," came Samantha's reply, "I guess you've some undercover reason for returning, too?"

Clare gave a light explanation that she might be helping someone but steered clear of any detail. She was aware of how leaky the whole network around Westminster was.

She arrived early, but and was surprised to see both Serena and Maggie already in the office. They looked pleased to see Clare, but almost immediately Maggie asks, "So what's the angle this time? – So that we can help you, of course!"

Clare answers, "There seems to be more clandestine lobbying. This time it is away from Andrew -- Thank

God - and apparently it is quite targeted."

"Well, I had a phone call from one of your supporters early this morning," says Serena, "From Amanda Miller. She said you didn't' know she was calling ahead, but that she wanted to underwrite that you'd have similar support to the last time."

Clare looks startled. Amanda Miller ran a department in SI6 - the security services - and they had worked together on a couple of assignments, with her associates from The Triangle. Amanda liked the ability to use reliable 'off books' people to assist with her investigations.

"No, you are right, I didn't have any knowledge of this, and I can't work out how Amanda would even know that I was coming back here!"

She thought back over her outgoing calls from Jake's. One must have been picked up. Jake, Lottie and Tessa, or Rachel. It had to be Rachel's phone that had been intercepted. A well-known investigative journalist with good access to Parliament. It had to be - but it was stranger that Rachel didn't realise.

She decides to meet Rachel in Parliament's cafe to warn her of a possible phone hack and texts Rachel to set it up.

Clare hurries through the underground tunnel to the Jubilee Café and to her surprise Rachel is already there, sitting at a corner table, which Clare reckons would have a good view of most of the room.

"Old habits?" she says as they meet, waving her arm around the room.

"Oh, I see what you mean. Just sometimes it is useful to see who is talking to whom. Case in point, that's the Energy secretary talking to his opposition number. There is probably some kind of a deal going down - one they want people to know about."

"I see, otherwise it would be somewhere far more discreet?" asks Clare.

"Yes, you have learned his place fast, Ms Crafts!" smiles Rachel.

"I wanted to warn you about something," says Clare, "I think you have been hacked."

Rachel looked interested, "How so?" she asks.

"I only told a handful of people about my staying on, yet by today everyone seems to know about it. I worked out that there can only be a few people who could be the source, however unwittingly, of the leak."

Rachel smiles, "Yes, that'd be my leaky phone," She delves into her voluminous Mulberry and plucks out a handset. "This one - my iPhone. Did I ever tell you I have an iPhone and a MyPhone? They can be very useful in situations like this."

Rachel rummages further into her bag and produced a second iPhone. This one was red.

"See, I have two phones. Only very few people ever make it to the red one."

"So, you knew we'd be overheard?" asks Clare.

"Intercepted, more like. This is how it stacks up. I'm an investigative reporter who stumbles across secrets. Who wants to know? Amanda Miller and her friends along at Vauxhall Cross. It's so much better when they discover a new tidbit. It keeps them comfortable thinking that they are monitoring me."

"But why now?"

"Despite the demise of Medusa, it is still a boom time for lobbyists. Although the Prime Minister pretends to squash lobbying, especially by Ministers and Members, he still knows what he is doing. Rush a Bill through and leave the edges ripe for a thousand unintended consequences. You only have to blend in the normal warp and weft of parliamentary business and then the actions of any specific MP disappear into a void of diary and note management: 'I can't remember. I don't recollect.' They are useful statements if ever anything approaches a Hearing."

Clare notices that Rachel looks tired.

"Let's just say that Duncan Melship gets that new

Ministerial post. Department for Transport Efficiency- DfTE. No one will have time to check his background credentials nor have much of a mind to do so. And anyway, they can soon float that DfTE is quite like DAFT, so here will be any number of puns and silly pictures flying around."

"I see, the usual thing where distraction is used as a cover-up," agrees Clare.

"Are you sure you haven't done this role before?" asks Rachel, "I mean before you turned up at Andrew's doorstep?"

"Well, it's handy because I know Duncan Melship quite well. My ex-flatmate Lottie is his Assistant and she invited me along to a few of his bashes," answers Clare.

"Hmm, you know about his - er - wandery hands?" asks Rachel, looking slightly surprised.

"Yes, and so does everyone else on the inside of Parliament," answers Clare, "But he does throw a good and rather lavish celebrity bash, and I can normally tell quite quickly whether it is worth staying."

Rachel points to her lanyard, "See the brown badge. That's what stops me from getting to most of those events. Your green one tells a whole different story."

"Yes, but you are savvy and know how to tap information, " said Clare, smiling, "And I'm sure you can expense the odd lunch or two? I guess some of those middle-aged men will be forming a line to get away from school dinners to have lavish lunch with a glamorous member of the fifth estate?"

Rachel laughs, "Yes, however harrowing the experience might be!" Then she gathers her Mulberry and the two phones. "Right, I'm moving now, but it is good to know that SI6 considered me worthy of intercepts. You'd better not tell Amanda about my second phone though."

Clare made like she was zipping her mouth.

"Always a pleasure," she says, "Although I guess we'd better not be seen together too much or someone will infer something."

"See, I knew you were good!" smiles Rachel as they hug and then Rachel leaves the Caffè.

Before Clare has a chance to move, there is a loud noise behind her, and she turns to see Lottie and Tessa giggling towards her.

"What are you hiding, Clare? You leave one day, return the next - typical Clare I might add," says Lottie.

"Then the very next day we see you with super-journalist/investigator Rachel Crosby. There has to be something going on?" adds Tessa.

"No, we were just catching up on the outcome from

that Medusa thing. All those MP's being persuaded to lobby because of their little indiscretions."

"It sounds like the whip system to me," says Lottie, "Men behind the men who vote, telling them how to think."

"Not always men," says Clare.

"No but mostly men as whips," says Lottie, "Except for Ann, Jacquie and Hilary over the years, maybe - but you get the picture."

"But have you heard the latest?" asks Lottie, "My MP Duncan Melship is to be the Secretary of State in the new Department for Transport Efficiency- DfTE. It's such a shame that the newspapers are already using headlines like 'DAFT Appointment of Melship to new role' and they are already calling him Daft Duncan. It is so unfair."

Clare senses the irony in Lottie's tone as she relays this information.

Tessa speaks, "But think of all the new parties! and with automobiles come even bigger celebrity personal appearances!"

"We are going to need a crash course in cars!" says Clare.

They all laugh and Tessa continues, "Everyone knows about Duncan Melship's parties and no-one wonders where he finds the money to throw them.

Now he has a whole new source."

Lottie says, "I'll wait for all of the new invitations for Duncan to speak and attend various functions. He will be sure to choose wisely."

"But back to the central question," says Tessa, "Clare, you are still working for Andrew Brading, but must have something else going on in parallel? What is it - you know we want to help."?

"All in good time," says Clare, "For now I want to ensure that Andrew Brading's next Bills get through the Commons in an unadapted form!"

Clare realises that she would need a cover story to tell Tessa and Lottie. She knows from experience they could be very persistent.

I'm in love with my car

The machine of a dream
Such a clean machine
With the pistons a pumpin'
And the hubcaps all gleam
When I'm holding your wheel
All I hear is your gear
With my hand on your grease gun
Oooh, it's like a disease, son

I'm in love with my car
Got a feel for my automobile
Get a grip on my boy-racer rollbar
Such a thrill when your radials squeal
Told my girl I'd have to forget her
Rather buy me a new carburettor
So, she made tracks, saying
"This is the end now"
"Cars don't talk back"
"They're just four-wheeled friends, now"

When I'm holding your wheel
All I hear is your gear
When I'm cruisin' in overdrive
Don't have to listen
To no run-of-the-mill talk jive

Roger Meddows Taylor

43

Triangle office

The next morning Clare made her way on the Jubilee Line around to the offices of The Triangle. These were situated along the South Bank in an area known as Hay's Galleria.

They had acquired a small space in the property after the destruction of their prior offices in Hoxton. The new building was well-equipped and conveniently situated for their trips around London and was not too far from any of their apartments.

'Hiya," said Bigsy as Clare walked in, "The gang's all here!"

She looked over and saw Jake talking to Christina, who had been a late addition to the original trio of Jake, Clare and Bigsy. Christina was a star acquisition - literally - she had been the main singer for a pop act. She also possessed a complex background, being borne in Iceland, but later recruited to the GRU in Russia and trained in Saint Petersburg and Bulgaria. After many missions, she had bought her way out, but everyone knew that the Kremlin would still regard her as a deep asset in London.

"Hey babe, " said Christina to Clare. They hugged, "You are staying on? There's still more to do at Parliament. - Surely not?"

They both laughed. Jake called them into a glass meeting room. It was a 'Bigsy special', which he'd set up so that no radio waves would be able to get inside.

"Westminster bubble-schmubble. It won't beat this one," said Jake.

"Okay, now we are secure, I can tell you what I know," said Clare.

"Rachel tipped me off that there is still some kind of influence strategy running around Parliament. She thinks it is the reason her brother David was killed a year ago. It seems to be somehow independent from the Medusa set-up, which used simple blackmail to get what they wanted. This seems to be more monetarily operated."

"I'll ask around my contacts," said Christina, "But I doubt even the Kremlin would try the same thing for the third time!"

Jake added, "And Duncan Melship has just taken up a new position as a Minister - for something called Department for Transport Efficiency. I can't help wonder if there is a connection?"

Tessa added, "And Melship knows nothing about cars. Except how to sit in the back of them."

Clare shook her head, "That would be almost too convenient, given my link with Lottie, who is his Research Assistant! More interesting is that Amanda knew about me staying on, and I can only conclude that MI6 somehow hacked Rachel's phone to intercept this information."

"It is a clever hack, too, to be able to find the exact usable information so quickly. It seems to me that someone has been watching Rachel for a while," said Christina.

"We should ask Amanda," said Jake, "I don't think she'll have forgotten how helpful we have been to her in the past."

With that, Jake picked up his phone and dialled Amanda Miller's cell phone.

"Foreign ringtone," he said, "She must travelling,"

"Oh, Hello Amanda! I hope you are well?"

They could all hear the background of Amanda talking, but Jake didn't put it on speaker, so they only heard half the conversation.

"Really? I've never been there - Helsinki."

"Yes, yes, in our office, together."

"We wanted to ask you something..."

 "Okay, no, we will."

"So, Clare had been asked to stay on in Parliament. But we think you knew that already. We think there is still some untoward lobbying occurring. Not connected with the previous scams. We wondered how you knew so quickly. We think you found out from Rachel?"

"Indirectly?"

"Could it have been by your phone intercept?"

"And why the interest? Are you following this one too?"

"You are?"

"Proposition? I'll need to explain it to the others."

He listened for a few minutes whilst Amanda explained her idea.

"Everyone. It's a similar setup to last time - working with Amanda - Are we all in?"

Bigsy and Christina nodded and Clare raised both her thumbs, all to signify 'yes'.

"Okay, it's a yes from us. Next time we call we'd

better all be secure."

"Oh, you are secure? Of course, you would be!"

"*Moi-Moi*, Amanda, *Moi-Moi*!"

Jake turned back to the others. "I should really have put that on speaker phone, but I didn't want to put her off."

He looked at Clare. "You were right about Amanda tracing Rachel's phone. And she is interested in this new form of sleaze. Amanda thinks it is something that a few MPs have invented by themselves. Not a state actor in sight, although she thinks it could be a corporate player. However, she wants to nip it in the bud before it blossoms into something unsightly. Amanda says that the whips are useless on this situation. They only want to deal in their own forms of moral suasion, not have ones imposed from outside sources. Self-interest at its finest."

Christina added, "And if your so-called corporate actors discover that this is happening, then they will want to leverage the situation. You have to assume they are in the picture somewhere."

Clare grinned, she looked happy that she had guessed most of it.

Jake spoke, "I've an idea that could help us move this forward. Remember I used to work for Street?"

Clare nodded.

Jake continued, "And that we did items about 'flash-boys' who drove fancy cars? You remember, like Darren Collins? Well, our car expert there was a chap called Tony Brooklands. He knows everything about cars. We used to be great buddies. I could get him to come over to the office and to provide us with a briefing."

"But will he know the kind of thing we are interested in?" asked Clare., "I don't want someone who is a car-bore. You know - someone who can tell us how many horsepower we can get from a Mini-Cooper and likes watching middle aged blokes drive multi-coloured sports cars around racetracks. You know the kind of fella. They are often seen in bars."

"Oh yes, like Toad of Toad Hall? No - I'd say that Tony is about as far from Toad as you can get. Leave it with me."

Lady driver

Duncan Melship was delighted. He had expected to stay resolutely on the backbenches, but this was now his chance! A Secretary of State. He'd be on news segments. He'd probably get some TV spots on 'The Answers' and maybe even some fun appearances on those alternative TV shows. And a Jaguar. Being driven around in a Jaguar. No worries about where to park and always being picked up by his driver.

"Can you check that for me?" he asks Lottie, "If possible, I'd like a female driver for my Jaguar. I'll be one of the top 20 MPs after this so I don't think I should settle for a Pool driver."

Lottie looks at some of the new policy documents in preparation. Somewhat starkly it was presenting the new MP code of conduct for travel.

"It says you'll be using an electric car unless on a very long journey. The PM has also let it be known that it is best for you to have your private vehicle as an electric too. He wants to avoid negative publicity. In fact, he wants this done quickly so you can issue some immediate positive press releases."

She handed across an A4 sheet. It listed the top 10 all-electric vehicles, with notes next to each one about their country of origin. It looked as if he would have to settle for a Sunderland manufactured e-car instead. It didn't have a very English sounding name and Melship thought it was from the far east.

"Hold on though. Don't Jaguar make an electric car? An SUV?" Asked Melship.

"They make hybrids," explains Lottie, "They are on another list entirely."

"So, what is the difference?" asks Melship.

"They still have petrol or diesel engines inside," explains Lottie, scanning a car brochure from the internet, "They are only partly electric."

"Hmm," says Melship, " I can see there are some downsides with all this climate saving,"

"I think we'd better get you briefed on recent car developments," answers Lottie.

Above the fold

The next day, Duncan Melship makes the newspapers. He was standing next to a plain-looking electric car, surrounded by manufacturer-supplied smiling, pretty women. The announcement described his new post and that he had already changed his Ministerial car to an all-electric model and had plans to do the same with his private vehicle.

"It's a triumph!" says Melship to Lottie, "Look I'm above the fold on several of the papers and the lead story in a couple! And I've already had several helpful people contact me about transport infrastructure briefings."

Lottie looks at the list of offers. It was like a rollcall of the major manufacturers. She has never been this close to blatant lobbying before.

"But I think we have to turn these down," she says to Melship, "They are a little close to briefing jollies."

"Obviously some of them are trying to take a chance,

but I've noticed that several mention that they could provide briefings at the upcoming auto industry Expo. Obviously, I'd need support if I went to that and it is entirely within my purview."

Lottie's mind struggles with this idea. "I suppose if you arrange your own transport and then overtly choose the specific sessions then it might work. Where is it?"

Melship smiles, "Oh, I think it is abroad somewhere - Let me look again, oh yes, it says Gstaad, Switzerland."

Lottie asks, "But that's the Swiss Alps. Most people go there for skiing or to be jet-setters?"

"I know, but the car industry is using it to make a point. There is a main car show in Geneva and then a special satellite Expo two and a half hours away, where they show the latest SUVs and long-range electric cars."

"Does the PM know about this?" asks Lottie.

"Oh, I told him I was going to Geneva on a fact-finding visit. He was entirely supportive. It is accurate as well, my flights are in and out of Geneva, but I'm being met and driven to the Expo from the main show."

Lottie realised that Melship was taking full advantage of his new position.

"Oh yes and they have asked me to present something at the Gstaad Expo. I'll need your help with that."

Colour drains from Lottie's face.

Amanda calls

Back at Parliament, Clare's mobile rang. 'Amanda,' it said.

She picked up. "Hi Amanda," she could hear the soundscape of an airport.

"Sorry, I've just been through security," said Amanda, "But this is my best chance to call you."

"And where are you today?" asked Clare.

"On my way back, via Stockholm, then to LHR. I should be back to T4 by around 8 pm, " answers Amanda, "Look we've been delving into the lobby situation. There's nothing obvious this time. The biggest move I can see is around that new appointment - you know - Duncan Melship to be Secretary of State for - what is it? - Department for Transport Efficiency."

"Yes, we had noticed this as well," answers Clare.

"Well, it sounds as if there's a couple of big players ready to pitch in," continues Amanda, "They have offered Melship various trips to a Swiss Car Expo but he has turned them down. He wants to be seen to have made his own way to Geneva."

"Geneva?" asks Clare.

"Well not exactly. The main briefings are in Geneva but the electric Car Expo is another two and a half hours away in Gstaad. We can get you tickets to both parts of the Exposition, but you'll need to make your own flight and accommodation arrangements. It's not until the New Year, when the Swiss snow is pretty much guaranteed."

"Never a dull moment!" answers Clare.

"And no links back to me," asks Amanda above the sound of plane announcements.

Clare had just hung up the call when Lottie appeared in the doorway of the office.

"Lottie?" exclaims Clare, "Wow - a visit! It must be serious."

Lottie looks at Clare, "I need some help," she says, "I think you can provide it, only I wouldn't usually ask but this is a big deal for Duncan and I don't want to mess up."

"What is it?" asks Clare, "Come on sit down." They were alone in Andrew Brading's office.

"Duncan Melship made that Press Release about using an electric car today. I talked to him some more and it is evident that he knows next to nothing about cars and I'm afraid he will say something ill-advised."

"I need some kind of briefing so that I can keep him on the right track until he goes to a trade show in a few weeks' time."

"Lottie, this is your lucky day! My company is just arranging a briefing from Tony Brooklands the automobile journo. Jake knows him well and we are running it from our office. Why don't you come on over? You can meet the gang and you'll be bound to pick up some useful knowledge."

Lottie answered, "The thing is, we need the Department to be squeaky clean - no lobbying or bribery or anything. You should know this from that last business you were mixed up in."

"Lottie, we'll be squeaky clean. Don't worry! Just come along and take away as much knowledge as you can hold. You know what - bring Tessa as well so you've a good alibi and witness."

Tony Brooklands

Jake had called his ex-colleague and Tony duly arrived at The Triangle offices, and to Clare's relief didn't look like a typical middle-aged motor journalist. Before she sized him up fully, Christina had already whispered in Clare's ear, "He's got the body of a Formula 1 driver, trust me."

Lottie and Tessa had both come along. As well as the electric car briefing, they were both intrigued to see the other place Clare worked, and to meet some of her colleagues.

Lottie smiles across to Tony and then he gave a dazzling smile back across all of them. Tessa whispers, "Clare, you are always full of nice surprises."

Tony could sense the attention and playfully removes his leather jacket.

"Okay now, Jake tells me you need to know something about electric cars? Would someone like to explain?"

"We are helping some people in the government," explains Clare blandly, "but need to be further ahead of the marketplace in terms of our understanding. We are hoping you can provide us with that briefing as well as any personal opinions you might hold about the options."

"Ah, okay; Jake said it would be like a brain dump," he breezily replies, looking towards Jake, "It is lucky that I was talking to the Society of Motor Manufacturers on this exact topic. 'E-cars and their infrastructure' - I brought the slides." He opens a small MacBook and looks for somewhere to plug it into. Bigsy steps forward with a small box and connects everything together.

"These slides are not confidential, nor are they proprietary, but I'd ask you not to pass them on further," Tony begins.

"Say, if you want to find out about the automobile industry you should all go to the Geneva Car Fair. It is supposed to be 'Trade Only' but I'm sure that someone with Jake's resourcefulness can get you all passes."

"We are ahead of you, for once," says Jake, "We are already ticketed!"

"Wow, I haven't even got my ticket yet - but I guess I'll see you all there!" replies Tony.

"Okay Slide One - A Summary" He presses a button and the slide advances.

"Let's remind ourselves: The UK has committed to Net-Zero carbon emissions by 2050."

He continues, "Transport is currently the largest emitting sector of the UK economy, responsible for 27% of total UK greenhouse gas emissions. Within this, cars are responsible for 55% of transport emissions. The UK Government has just appointed a Duncan Melship to lead the initiatives around this area. He heads a new Department called Department for Transport Efficiency- DfTE. You've probably seen it mentioned in the news over the last couple of days."

They all nod, realising that Jake had not told Tony who they worked for.

Tony continues, "Electric vehicles (EVs, sometimes known as Ultra Low Emission Vehicles (ULEVS)) offer one method of reducing emissions, with the Committee for Climate Change (CCC) suggesting that all new vehicles should be electrically propelled by 2035, if not sooner, to achieve the Net Zero target."

"You'd better explain what an EV and a Hybrid is," says Jake.

Tony smiles and puts up the next slide.

"What are EVs? EVs run, either partially or wholly,

on electricity, stored on board the vehicle in batteries or produced from hydrogen. Whilst cars represent 92% of the 432,000 ULEVS licensed (1.1% of all licensed vehicles) at the end of 2020, there are also electric motorcycles, taxis, buses, vans, and heavy goods vehicles.

"The market for EVs is immature, yet growing, with 8.5% of UK registered vehicles ULEVs in 2020. Meanwhile, only 1.8% of used car sales, responsible for approximately 80% of transactions, involved alternatively fuelled vehicles."

And we'd like to know what the government is doing to support all of this?" asks Lottie.

Tony smiles again, "You are a good audience and know all the right questions to ask," He flicks to the next slide.

"Government measures in support of EVs: There have been a variety of strategies employed over the past decade to encourage the uptake of EVs. Since 2011, the Government have supported EV ownership through the plug-in grant scheme. Additionally, the Government plans to ban the sale of new diesel and petrol cars and vans from 2030, whilst only fully zero-emission vehicles will be sold from 2035. This will require significantly increased battery numbers, opening up the potential for the UK to develop battery production facilities."

"And batteries are still a big issue?" asks Clare.

"Yes, UK can't make enough, the technology is like a phone battery and runs down. The last 20% is difficult to charge and they degrade with use, maybe with a life of 5 to 8 years. At present, they also make up to between 40% and 50% of the cost of an EV."

Christina adds, "An example to generate sales: In Russia, the Russian government offers subsidies to manufacturers of electric vehicles and batteries to co-finance the costs associated with the construction of plants and to special investment contracts. Electric cars can drive free of charge on toll roads. As a further incentive, electric cars are to be included in concessionary loan and leasing programmes."

Clare speaks, "That seems strange, with Russia presiding over some of the world's largest oil resources?

Christina replies, "Moscow's push for electric mobility is simply driven by the global market. Like the way Russia plays the energy markets. It is the irony of the way the Russians nowadays like to follow the money."

Tony continues, "Well, getting back to the UK, the Government produced the 'Transport Decarbonisation Plan,' to cover all road vehicles as well as the rail, aviation and freight sectors. I guess that will be an ongoing project for some time."

Lottie looks at her notes.

"What about electricity demand?" she asks.

Tony smiled, "Now you've caused me to go out of sequence! Just a moment." He smiles as he fiddles with the computer, "Here we are - Electricity Demand: Currently, road transport uses approximately 500 Tera Watt hours of energy.

"Although improved efficiencies may reduce this, the shift from petrol and diesel cars could increase electricity demand by 200 Tera Watt hours. That's a lot! The use of smart charging or vehicle to grid technologies could significantly lower peak demands to be approximately only 8% greater than current peak power draw."

"So are EVs the silver bullet then?" asks Lottie, "Will they help save the planet from carbon's environmental impact?"

Tony answers, "No slide for this, but my opinion...EVs improve local air quality and reduce point-of-use emissions; however, they are not net-zero when considering the whole life cycle of a vehicle and its sub- components, as well as the particulate matter emitted on-street."

"Further, batteries for EVs can require rare elements such as lithium and cobalt, which has raised environmental and ethical issues in countries where these elements are mined. There are also concerns over 'peak lithium' and future shortages constraining growth in the EV market."

Tony continues, "It brings me to my next topic: Why do we need Electric Vehicles? "

He was back into his slide sequence.

"As of 2019, transport was the largest-emitting sector of the UK economy at 122 mega tonnes carbon dioxide equivalent (MtCO2e), accounting for 27% of total UK greenhouse gas (GHG) emissions. Of this, cars represented the greatest proportion of emissions within the transport sector in 2019, accounting for 55% of transport emissions."

"So, all of these stories about cows and methane and suchlike?" asks Jake.

Tony continues, "The story and statistics are very garbled on livestock. Not to mention the transport lobby's effect. Past and current governments have supported measures to encourage uptake of EVs as they can contribute to a wide range of transport policy goals. For example, EVs can help to improve air quality, reduce noise pollution and support efforts to reduce carbon emissions."

"So now there is a greater push for electric vehicles, like the 'dash for diesel', back when Gordon Brown was the PM?" asks Jake.

Tony nods, "Exactly. Millions of Britons switched to drive very polluting vehicles, while being told it was less damaging to the environment. Emissions of nitrogen oxides and particulates were linked to respiratory difficulties, heart attacks and lung cancer. It was - is - an unsurfaced scandal."

Then he continues, "But beyond the diesel dash, the importance of EVs was outlined in updated advice on meeting the net zero 2050 target, published in May 2019 by the Committee on Climate Change (CCC) – the statutory advisors on emissions reductions for Government. This said that the market for electric cars and vans should scale up to 100% of new sales by 2035 at the latest (and ideally by 2030) to meet the net zero target."

"Can we believe any of this, given the government's abject performance on diesels?" asks Clare.

"When it is all couched in terms of 'pathways' and other management speak, I'd say it was dubious."

Christina adds, "What is it they say? 'It always works in PowerPoint?'"

Tony continues, "So, to my point, under the older 80% reduction target by 2050, the CCC advised a 'least cost' pathway would need 60% of all new cars and vans sold to be electric by 2030. Management consultancy speak if ever I heard it."

"And don't forget, although electric vehicles offer "clear benefits" for local air quality due to zero exhaust emissions at street level, they still emit particulate matter from road, tyre and brake wear. This means EVs cannot entirely eliminate issues of air pollution in cities."

"Further, they do not address wider issues, such as urban sprawl, inactive lifestyles, or congestion, which may increase due to reduced operational costs of motoring. The CCC has recommended that if the UK is to meet the 2050 net zero target, 100% of new vehicle sales should be electrically propelled by 2035 at the latest (and ideally by 2030)."

"So, has someone got a number in an envelope in a drawer?" asks Jake, smiling.

"You'll have to ask the new man, Duncan Melship, although I've never seen him in any remote connection with the automobile industry up to this point," answers Tony.

"As an example, progress in reducing emissions in the transport sector has been slow. In 2018 the average CO_2 emissions of newly registered vehicles was 124.9 grams per kilometre (g/km).

"This is down from 178.8 g/km in 2001 and represents a decrease of around 30%. Between 2001 and 2018 the average CO_2 emissions of newly registered vehicles were falling year on year although this then began to rise again from mid-2016. "

"But were some of those numbers faked?" asks Lottie, "Remember the various car scandals about rigging the system to show lower emissions that were actually occurring?"

Tony nods, "Sadly so, and the Americans are running all kinds of class actions about the misrepresentation."

Drily he adds, "And I'm not sure all that many people study the emissions when they are buying their next car. More to do with capacity for ferrying the kids to school or looking good in the car park."

"This is good stuff," says Lottie, who had been taking copious notes, "Can we get your slides too?"

Tony looks at Jake, "I guess so, although I'd need to anonymise them first. But we are on to the next piece. The Road to Zero."

Road to Zero

Tony continues, "Way back in 2009, the Labour Government published its ULEV strategy. It said it would provide £20 million "seed money" to support the development of lead cities and regions in building the necessary charging infrastructure to help increase consumer confidence that would make ultra-low carbon vehicles viable. The Strategy also expected the private sector ultimately to take the lead in infrastructure provision.

"Then the Labour manifesto for the 2010 General Election promised to 'ensure there are 100,000 electric vehicle charging points by the end of the next Parliament'."

Tony grimaces, "It's bunkum, of course. The stats to the end of 2021, show that there were around 48,000 charging points on 28,000 devices at 18,000 locations. Like with everything else, the government can blame the pandemic."

"What happened after that? That all seems to be Labour government policy?" asks Lottie.

"Enter the Coalition," says Tony, " They committed

to 'mandate a national recharging network for electric and plug-in hybrid vehicles'. In the June 2011 EV infrastructure strategy, they said the approach was not to mandate 'a ChargePoint on every corner'. Rather, it said most of the recharging is likely to take place at home and at work, so an extensive public recharging infrastructure would be under-utilised and uneconomic.

Tony continues, "Labour said at the time that this represented a renege on the Coalition's commitment to a 'national charging network.' However, others, including manufacturers of electric vehicles, supported the Government's claim that most charging would be done at home or in the workplace and that the need for public recharging points was therefore limited. I happen to think they missed the long-distance driving aspect with this convenient simplification."

Tony smiles, "So then comes the humorously titled Road to Zero strategy."

"Talking Heads anyone?" says Jake, and he quietly sang

"We're on a road to nowhere
  Come on inside
  Takin' that ride to nowhere
  We'll take that ride"

"I know, the consultants they used for this strategy were having a laugh, weren't they? No wonder it is suspiciously low in the mix," replies Tony.

He continues, "The Government published its Road to Zero Strategy in 2018. It shows how the government intends to support the transition to zero emission road transport and reduce emissions from conventional vehicles during the transition. The strategy is 'long term in scope and ambition, considering the drivers of change, opportunities and risks out to 2050 and beyond'. It set out several new measures, including to phase out the sale of petrol and diesel vehicles, and the rollout of a charging infrastructure."

"But isn't that kicking the 2010 objective of 100,000 charging points further down the road?" asks Jake.

Tony answers, "Well spotted, and that's not the end of it. In March 2020 the Government issued a 'Decarbonising Transport: Setting the Challenge' report which details strategies to decarbonise transport, including those for road-based vehicles."

He continues, "It went on to say, '...we do not currently know the optimal path for delivering a decarbonised transport network. We, therefore, intend to work with business, academics, researchers and innovators, environmental NGOs and the wider public over 2020 to design the package of decarbonisation policies...'. Another kick of the can."

"Predictable, " says Clare. Lottie and Tessa both nod.

"Buying time," says Tessa.

Jake comments, "Buying time...Look at the time! We've been going for a couple of hours!"

Tony says, "Okay then, my final thought...Then a November 2020 paper confirmed that the Government would pursue a two-phased approach: Step 1 sees the phase-out date for the sale of new petrol and diesel cars and vans brought forward to 2030; and Step 2 sees all new cars and vans be fully zero emission at the tailpipe from 2035. The announcement said that hybrids could continue to be sold between 2030 and 2035 'if they have the capability to drive a 'significant distance' with zero emissions and this will be defined through consultation.' "

Tony smiles, "This is thirsty work; how about we adjourn to the pub and continue in a more relaxed format?"

Jockey full o' bourbon

Edna million in a drop-dead suit
Dutch pink on a downtown train
Two-dollar pistol but the gun won't shoot
I'm in the corner on the pouring rain

Yellow sheets on a Hong Kong bed
Stazybo horn and a slingerland ride
To the carnival is what she said
A couple hundred dollars makes it dark inside

Hey little bird, fly away home
Your house is on fire, your children alone
Hey little bird, fly away home
Your house is on fire, children alone

Tom Waits

Whiskey Sour

Clare arrives at the office the next morning with a sore head. She knew Jake could drink and normally Clare would be able to keep up, but this time the Whiskey sours had found their way through her defences.

It had been Tony's idea, although she soon realised, he couldn't even take the stuff he was suggesting. They had to pour him into a taxi at about nine-thirty in the evening, but then Jake had suggested 'one more for the road'.

If it was any consolation, she had remembered Lottie and Tessa were worse than her. The concoction of whiskey, lemon juice, sugar, and a dash of egg white with red wine floated on top, was ultimately lethal.

She sits down in a chair in the office and certain that her brain is suspended in alcohol which was taking more time to settle. She looks in the drawer and finds a pack of paracetamol, from which she dutifully takes a couple.

Her phone rings: it is Lottie.

"Hiya Babe," Lottie says, "Thank you so much for yesterday! It was great to get so much information so quickly."

Clare is surprised that Lottie sounds so chirpy after such an evening.

"My pleasure - we were drinking from the firehose, that's for sure."

"Yes, until it turned into boosted Whiskey!" says Lottie, "You know something? Tessa is a wreck this morning. I don't think she'll even go to work. She was huddled up on the sofa with 'Friends' on the telly when I left. I think it's the congeners or something."

"Oh yes, that thing about don't drink dark liquids; I remember that from my Uni days."

"And I remembered to drink about a pint of water when I got back. I tried to persuade Tessa but she was singing '99 Luftballon' in German - and making some of the original Nena moves!"

"Oh dear," said Clare, suddenly realising she was in better shape that she could have been. Although Lottie had certainly won on this occasion.

"Also, a quick 'heads up' from me that when you log on, you'll see the rumpus that Duncan has caused.

He's asking your MP Andrew for some assistance. Anyway - Later Babes!" And Lottie was gone.

Just at that moment, the door to the office opened. Serena appeared, "Oh. What happened? You look somewhat fragile. Almost into 'hair of the dog' territory, I'd say."

"Well spotted. I had rather an evening of it with some boys. They were drinking Sours."

"Oh, I've had the same with Singapore slings. Once experienced, but never forgotten. Look, have you seen the odd request from Duncan Melship? - He's passed it along to The State Secretary for Internal Affairs because he thinks he could save the day with it. It's the Aberdeen Pop-Up Chargers."

Clare has no idea what Serena is talking about.

Aberdeen Pop up chargers

To: Secretary of State for Internal Affairs

Andrew,

Here's an interesting idea, maybe our departments could work together to come up with something like this across the UK?

Duncan

Secretary of State for Department for Transport Efficiency- DfTE

Attachment: (Article)

Aberdeen installs pop-up EV chargers in pilot project ahead of 2030 ban on new petrol and diesel cars

Along Aberdeen's Union Street, two businessmen in suits stride along the street avoiding a slower moving assembly of tourists with wheely bags. The suitcases roll over a row of electric vehicle chargers, and the tourists barely notice their existence.

Unlike bulkier on-street chargers, which draw complaints for clogging up pavements, these "pop up" devices only appear when activated using an app. "A lot of people walk past they don't realise they are there," said Angus Crombie, corporate fleet manager at Aberdeen city council, which is involved in a £5.2m project to test 36 pop-up chargers throughout the city.

Whether the UK will have sufficient charging facilities to meet the government's 2030 ban on new petrol and diesel cars and vans has recently become a subject of deep concern among MPs and policymakers. Aberdeen was chosen for this new initiative because of its close associations with North Sea oil.

The government has already confirmed legislation to ensure that all new homes are built with a charging point but EV experts say the bigger hurdle will be providing sufficient facilities for the estimated 8m-plus households that do not have access to a driveway in which to install their own device.

More than 10 times the current number of public devices, estimated at more than 25,000, would be needed by the end of the decade, warned the Competition and Markets Authority in July.

MPs also said in a damning report in May that they were "not convinced" ministers had "sufficiently thought through" how to expand charging infrastructure "at the pace required."

In 2019, Scotland agreed a 2045 net zero emissions target, five years ahead of the wider UK 2050 deadline.

With projects such as the pop-up EV chargers, Aberdeen has become something of a laboratory to learn how cities can meet the 2030 ban. The council said it had already installed sufficient public facilities to charge almost 10 per cent of the cars and vans passing through the city.

The same percentage for the rest of the UK falls to just 1.9 per cent. But it becomes difficult for local authorities to understand how much costly infrastructure is needed and in which locations, particularly as the technology was changing so rapidly.

EV charging provision is not a statutory duty for local authorities and councils' enthusiasm and skills for the task can vary wildly, according to Robert McHenry, head of e-strategy at Metropolix, a consultancy involved in the pop-up chargers project.

"Because EV chargers are new, they find a different home in every local authority. In some local authorities, it's the fleet section. Some places it's the highways team, in some places it's the sustainability team," said McHenry.

Private companies have engaged in an early battle for market share. Major oil companies have offered to install tens of thousands of on-street chargers in the UK by 2025. One oil major has offered to assist local authorities in England with their share of installation costs to accelerate the rollout. The move was seen by analysts as part of a "land grab" by energy and utilities for prime charging locations, which tend to be in large cities and wealthier urban locations, leaving charging "deserts" in other areas, such as north-west England.

Even though it was "really hard to make money at the moment" from charging networks, said McHenry, companies were "positioning themselves" to control prime locations. "In 10 years', time when the numbers of EVs go up that's worth a lot of money and they are in control of the assets."

A spokesperson for the Department for Transport Efficiency believes charging provision should be included in council's statutory duties, and funding for specialist "charging officers" should be part of future settlements between central government and local authorities. Councils should "bundle" packages of charging locations to ensure that private networks do not pick off prime areas and leave rural and underprivileged communities unserved, according to the group.

The CMA found in its July report that, of 5,700 on-street charge points in place in the UK, only 1,000 were outside London. Drivers' costs and the way in which charging is paid for, often requiring different apps or cards, varies wildly between networks.

Experts fear this could become a barrier to further take-up of electric vehicles. The CMA warned that "local monopolies" of charging networks could also develop "if left unchecked."

But McHenry believes fears about the number of public chargers needed are overblown. Secretary of State for Internal Affairs research suggests half of drivers use their car so little they typically would only need to fully charge their vehicle twice a month. A 'Clear Streets' campaign spokesperson William Dacre said, "People often imagine that what we need is rows of chargers along every street in which cars are parked. The reality is EVs don't need charging that often. We don't need a charge point outside everybody's home."

Clare giggles as she reaches the end of the article. It was helping her lift the fog from her brain.

"Boys' toys?" asks Serena, "Or a practical solution?"

"More things to go wrong," answers Clare, "Even the hire-bikes in London have their share of mechanical, electrical and payment failures. Imagine that when the meters are underground and must be powered to the surface with electric motors. How many pigeons will get inside? And rodents? Oh sorry, I think it is the hangover speaking."

Serena smiles, "No, I happen to think you are right. Putting the charge points under crowded pavements means that they are not in the way when they are not in use. Imagine the same procession of tourists with wheeled luggage traversing the street when the units have surfaced and there are cables connected to cars. A pure case of first-level thinking.

"So, we will need to manage the new-found enthusiasm of Duggie."

Clare realises it was this that Lottie had been warning her about. She was thankful for the extra knowledge imparted yesterday by Tony.

Travel brochures

Lottie was in Duncan Melship's office. He was avidly reading a couple of travel brochures.

"They sent these with some admission tickets for a couple of special events," he says.

"Do you notice that they have kept the business section of the itinerary separated from the leisure section?"

Lottie smiles as she realises why this has been done.

"I guess it makes it easy to submit a business case for attending," she says, "without referencing the Gala Ball, the ski chalet bases for attendees and the sports car drive to the venue. Come to think of it, it doesn't even mention the fireworks display."

"No, none of them!" says Melship, "I see they are doing one display over the lake in Geneva and another one against the mountains, complete with a torchlight procession!"

"And each of the tables for the Gala Ball is hosted by a celebrity. There's dozens: film, music, sport, even television."

Lottie looks through the list. The tables were priced at different levels according to the celebrity hosting it. She wondered whether Melship had even noticed this aspect. Then she spotted a name she recognised. Jallie T. She knew Jallie T. was a friend of Clare's and Christina's.

"Leave it with me," says Lottie, "I'm sure I can - er - explain our various selections. Just don't be too extravagant or you'll get picked up by the paparazzi."

Lottie was already dialling Clare.

"Hiya Clare, I remember your friend Christina was a pop star. Didn't she tour with Jallie once?"

Clare replies, "Yes, we both did, all around the world: Russia, Japan, the USA, I'd say she became a lifelong friend of both of us!"

Lottie sighs, "You are doing it again, Clare, showing me that you have an ever-increasing list of surprises. Can I ask for some more help?"

"Sure, my hangover is now diminishing!

"Well, Duncan Melship has been invited to a trade fair in Switzerland by several car manufacturers. He wants to go, and there's a whole hospitality programme to the side of the main event."

Clare laughs, "So it's a jolly really?"

"Duncan is overwhelmed with offers at present but seems to have his heart set on this particular session in Geneva and Gstaad."

"Gstaad? For a car show? Up all those mountains?"

"Don't even ask. But anyway, there is a Gala Ball at the event in Gstaad, which it seems only the great and the good get to attend. It has been set up with hosted tables and one of the hosts is Jallie T."

"Oh, I get it, you want me to fix it to get Melship on her table?"

"And that means me as well, please?"

"Let me call Jallie and see what is possible."

"Oh - Thank you, thank you, thank you!" says Lottie.

Another Table

Clare was in a taxi on her way back to her apartment. She called Jallie T and notices the foreign ring tone.

Clare speaks, "Hi Jallie - I hope you are well. Touring I guess?"

Jallie explains, "Yay- Clare! Yes, I'm in Brussels, touring with my band, mainly smaller venues, the tee-shirt listing looks more impressive than the actuality of it. Here- I'll read from one of the tee-shirts.

"Flekkefjord, Drammen and Sarpsborg in Norway, then then Switzerland to Berne, Rorschach, Appenzell, then to Germany, Stuttgart, Wuppertal, Hamburg, Frankenberg, Berlin, Rosenberg, Tübigen - wait for it - In Jan's Toolshed, then a bunch in Austria including Graz and Vienna and then back for the last few in Germany but finishing up in Brussels. It's been quite a trip. We'll be back at home for Christmas!"

"Whew, work it, babe."

"I know, but there's something to be said for those big arenas that you and Erebus could command with Christina. I think we'd have the equivalent of the first ten audiences in one of the arenas!"

"Anyway, I've called to ask you a favour?"

"Anything..."

"Well, I don't know if you know that you are doing a celeb appearance at a Car Fair yet? In Switzerland - Geneva/Gstaad?"

"Oh yes, I do actually, one of the car makers has said they will lend me a car for a year in return for attending it."

"Well, my favour is to ask you to request to sit with a few specific people."

"Hold on a minute, let me talk it over with Rishi, he's the band's manager nowadays."

"Rishi?" replies Clare, "Are you two...you know?"

"Yes, as a matter of fact, after that long tour with Christina, we got together. Darius was complaining anyway about his loss of control and we agreed to swap Rishi as the new Manager. He's very switched on - as well as very cute!"

"Okay, Okay, I guess he is within earshot?

"You got it. He's saying to me that they will be bound to want something in return. Wait a minute...He's suggesting that you offer Christina as another celeb on another table...That'd be amazing."

Clare considers it for about half a second. "Oh yes, we'll do it, and I'll be along as her PA or something. It would be brilliant to meet again."

"I'll start practicing Nirvana numbers again! We could do that 'teenage spirit' thing if they will let us!"

"Okay, I'll send over the details in an email, and send my love to Rishi - it will be great to see you all again!"

A visit to Lottie

Now, with the table deal confirmed, Clare decides to drop around to Lottie's office. It is in Portcullis House, the more modern part of the Parliament buildings, and it takes her around ten minutes to walk across.

She walks into an office bedecked with Xmas lights and a few cards pinned to one of the notice boards.

Lottie looka surprised and a couple of the other assistants look up when they see Clare, who was recognisable as the Research Assistant to Andrew Brading.

Lottie walks across the small office toward Clare and then nudges her into the corridor.

Clare speaks, "Okay, I've fixed it for Jallie T to be on Melship's table and we are negotiating the attendance of Christina Nott to host another table. That way I can get some extra people into the event."

"Whoa, you've got Christina as well. I imagine the car event promoters are chuffed!"

"Frankly it was a bartering chip to ensure that we could control Melship's table. Jallie T is getting a car for a year for showing up! - Anyway, the stage is now set!"

Xmas Party

The Department's Christmas Party is in full swing when Clare arrives. It's been done properly. Not just some smuggled-in wine in suitcases and Tesco nibbles. No, this is the real deal and at a hotel. The venue's entrance has been strung with fairy lights and tinsel. She wonders who is 'sponsoring' the event, but soon gets swept into the moment.

Each table has a small white board beside it, and Clare fears the worst - that party games have been included. There are crackers on the table and some are already wearing the cheap hats from inside the crackers.

A local school choir is singing in the entrance and there's mince pies upon entry and the option of mulled cider, or chilled prosecco. Clare decides to avoid anything that will mean she has less hands free.

Then to a table, where crackers are pulled. Jokes read out - not necessarily the ones from within the

Tom Thumb crackers.

The booze is now eggnog and punch but Clare continues with her hands-free rule.

Andrew Brading and Maggie are in a corner by plate-glass windows which look over a stark, brutalist courtyard which screams 'underground car park'. There is a low-level sleet in the grey evening which is fogging the view. Clare slips away from her designated table and joins them. They both look relieved that they will be able to sit with people they know.

She puts on a hat and reads the cracker joke out loud

"What do you get when you cross a snowman with a vampire? ... Frostbite"

Andrew laughs politely and then says:

"What does Santa get when he's stuck in the chimney? ... Claus-trophobia"

Maggie is sipping her eggnog and stares at the hazy view towards the River. She says, half-heartedly:

"Why is it getting harder to buy Advent calendars? ... Because their days are numbered"

Andrew is looking at the other party people in various stages of inebriation. One can sense that he must have a 'hands free' rule too, for such events.

Clare knows that Andrew's wife, Katherine is on a train heading back to their constituency home in Canmore Grenville. Andrew won't leave London until Christmas Eve, heading up on the train with a smattering of gifts from the House of Commons gift shop.

"Are you staying local? Or heading away?" asks Maggie, aware that they seldom have time for such small talk around the office.

"I'll be going back to Hampshire," says Clare, "A family get-together with party games, you know the kind of thing. And you?"

Maggie smiles, "My folk have a pile outside Durham. I'll be hunkering down there, although I expect we'll only have part of the house open."

Clare remembers that Maggie is from landed gentry. Probably Andrew, the Conservative MP, and State Secretary, will have the most modest Christmas of them all who share an office. Serena has already flown off to Normandy to take Christmas in her husband's rural French barn-conversion.

"I've never understood egg-nog. It's like drinking alcoholic custard."

"American," says Andrew. They all burst out laughing.

"No, I think it was the Brits actually," says Maggie, "They took a perfectly good posset and ruined it."

"I still love a good posset," said Andrew. They all laughed again. It was that end-of-term feeling finally creeping in.

"What's happening over there?" said Maggie. She nods sideways. Across the floor Douglas Lessiter is talking to a woman in her late twenties. He has a hand on her upper arm. She has her head down and is shaking her head, her face flushed.

"Does anyone know her?" Maggie asks. Lessiter glances around, like he can feel them looking, then he puts his face closer to the woman's, talking fast.

His grip is making the fabric of her suit jacket wrinkle. She moves her arm. Is she trying to pull away? It is hard to tell through the crowd.

"Only it looks nasty," says Maggie, standing as if to intervene.

Clare says, "I'll help" and they make their way to where Lessiter and the woman are standing. As they pass Maggie mimes recognition of the woman.

The woman moves and even through the crowd Andrew can see the reluctance with which Lessiter lets her go. Then everything has changed: Maggie and the woman are arm in arm and heading further towards the women's' powder room. Clare has peeled off and continues a conversation with

Duggie Lessiter to help ensure some distance, but then she explains that she must get back to Andrew.

Andrew looks around at the apparently happy colleagues raising a glass of Christmas cheer. A few are singing along with the carollers.

Then Maggie is coming back towards them carrying three cups of punch at once in a sort of triangular shape, with elbows out and biting the side of her lip as she concentrates.

"So?" Andrew asks. "How was the damsel in distress?"

"Didn't get much out of her," Maggie says. "I didn't try either, mind you. She seemed pretty shaken up. Something about a Non-Disclosure Agreement"

"She said she'd signed one. But she didn't mention her name. Anyway, she's gone home."

"She didn't tell you what Duggie was pressuring her about?" Andrew asks.

"No. She asked me to walk her out. Still, it gave me an excuse to get to the bar," Maggie shrugs and drinks her punch while Andrew examines his. It is neon red and has bits of what might be orange pith in it. He hopes it won't make the eggnog in everyone's stomach curdle.

Clare notices the phone, then the Parliament WhatsApp group and emails all go quiet.

An hour's drive back to Hampshire and a few days being part of the family. Time to decompress. She knows that Jake, Bigsy and Christina will be doing the same.

She realises that a way to get an awkward reputation is to keep sending emails at this time of year.

It is like a natural end to things, Samhain, Saturnalia and Yule leading to the New Year. A time to reflect before the sun cross wheel starts turning again.

Then a ping. It is from Amanda. "When are you back in London?" it asks. Clare is sure that Amanda must have way of tracing her all the way to Hampshire.

"4ᵗʰ Jan," replies Clare.

"Ok - let's meet. The Wolseley, Breakfast 5ᵗʰ Jan - 9am?"

"Agreed," replied Clare. "Developments," she thought.

Wolseley

Clare made her way through the well-heeled streets of St James, to the grandeur of the Wolseley restaurant.

It wasn't lost on her that Amanda had picked a venue that was once linked to the motor trade. Wolseley Motors Limited had wanted a prestigious car showroom in Mayfair at the site of 160 Piccadilly.

The English architect, William Curtis Green incorporated marble pillars and archways with Venetian and Florentine-inspired details, making for a grand and impressive building befitting of the company's ambitions.

Then, as it said on the menu, by 1926, the cars weren't selling as well as they had hoped and the firm went into bankruptcy. A bank took over the site and their new branch opened in the spring of 1927. The same architect was called upon once again to construct a banking counter and managers' offices either side of the main entrance, which today serve as the bar and tea salon.

From the early 21st Century, it became a restaurant but as testament to the longevity of Green's vision many aspects of his original design, such as the domed ceiling and monochrome geometric marble flooring, are still on view today.

'Great,' thinks Clare, 'to be sitting at one of the best breakfast spots in all of London.'

"Clare!" Amanda walks into the area in a shapely dark grey business-like jacket and skirt and they exchange hugs.

"Happy New Year," says Amanda.

"Happy New Year," responds Clare.

"I thought we should see in the New Year in style, hence the venue," explains Amanda. She leans forward, "And it will be easy to spot unexpected visitors in here."

"Are they yours?" asks Clare, pointing to a corner table where two men were fidgeting with croissants and coffee.

"Yes, and the one over there," she points to a lone woman enjoying a hot chocolate with a Müesli.

"Why so many?" asks Clare.

"I guess it's because I wanted to give them a treat!" confides Amanda, "Really - this could be just the two of us, but they have all done well during last year."

They both smile at this thought. Christina smiles also from the screened-off table behind Amanda.

"Okay, so what have we got then?" asks Clare, "I was intrigued with your sense of urgency."

"What we know and what we don't know," answers Amanda.

"To begin with, there are a couple of companies eager to pursue Melship when he is in Gstaad. They have both made strong bid to be on Jallie T's table. Oh, and by the way it was brilliant that you have managed to infiltrate it."

"Who are the companies?" asks Clare.

"One is that trillion-dollar electric car maker. The other is a relatively unknown startup called Zillian."

"We don't know what either of their agendas would be, but they are certainly different."

"There's also talk of some revaluation of Zillian before it goes public, but no one knows where this has come from."

"But wait, wasn't ZiL the name of an old Russian car manufacturer? They supplied the cars for many Russian leaders?" asks Clare.

"Yes, that thought didn't escape us either, and they did also make trucks with missile launchers and military buses, amongst other things. The cars were all as ugly as sin, by the way. Imagine stretched out versions of those big flat American looking cars and imagine them where curves are banned and all sheet metal has to be black and folded."

"Yuk - it sounds horrible. But you don't think there is any connection?"

"No, the company has been handled by Red Fox from Menlo Park."

"Menlo Park, that's where Facebook/Meta are based, isn't it?" asked Clare.

"Yes, but aside from Sand Hill Road - the investor playground, we cannot see any connection."

"So, what we know is that a couple of companies, one well-known and the other unknown, are going to be at the table with Duncan Melship in Gstaad."

"Correct - but I think we are on to something tangible now. We just need to keep following the thread."

Back to Bermondsey

A few days later, Clare was in a taxi to the old flat share in Bermondsey where she had lived with Lottie and Tessa. They had invited her over for a few glasses of new year celebratory wine.

As well as the opportunity for gossip, she would also be interested to meet the new occupant of her old room.

She climbed out of the taxi into a light sleet and scooted towards the front door. She rang the bell and a skinny long-haired woman in a checked shirt answered it.

"Oh Hi," says Clare, "I'm here to see Tessa and Lottie."

"Oh, come on in," answers the woman, "I'm Cat, and I guess you must be the oft-talked-about Clare? You work in Parliament as well, I gather?"

"Yes, that's right, but from that I'm thinking you

don't?"

"No, I'm a banker. I work for Corax Investments, in the city in their trading department."

"Oh - high finance and all of that?" asks Clare.

She was led into the lounge, which was unchanged from her time there and immediately Tessa and Lottie let off a confetti cannon, which sprinkled the room in glitter.

"There is always time for more glitter!" says Lottie.

"And surprises!" adds Clare. As she turned, she noticed a Christmas tree in the corner, complete with little lights.

"Nicely done!" says Tessa to Cat.

"Well, we'd better all have some bubbly after that!" says Lottie, " And welcome back, Clare."

They sit down with their glasses of Champagne and Clare notices a selection of other wine glasses and realises this could be quite an evening.

"So, Cat, how did you find out about this place?" asks Clare.

'Oh, I've known Tessa for years and she let me know that a spot was available. You might notice that I'm also originally from Germany. My full name is Katharina Maier, which does sound a little more

'Dgerman'. She emphasised a 'D' on the front of German in a pastiche of German pronunciation.

Until then, Clare hadn't noticed. Cat had a perfect Londoner accent.

"But I guess you are in my old room. It's not that large for an investment banker!"

"I agree, but I'm just starting out and this location - Bermondsey - is so convenient for everywhere. I can walk to the tube and be in Canary Wharf in about ten minutes.'

'The travel works for Corax Investments like it did for me travelling to Parliament," answers Clare.

"And the girls keep telling me about your various mysterious surprises. It's one of the reasons they wanted to ambush you," answers Cat.

"So, what's been happening with Duggie Melship over the last couple of weeks?" asks Clare looking at Lottie.

"Unbelievable!" answers Lottie. "Remember Melship was always one for parties and lavish surprises? Well, now he is involved with transport, there is an interesting amount on offer."

"Surely it has to be declared?" asks Clare.

"Yes and no; there are grey areas, like so much in politics. Remember that alleged Xmas Party at

Number 10 during lockdown? It is kind of like that."

Tessa interrupts, "Reality distortion."

Lottie laughs, then adds, "and ahem 'forgetfulness'. For example, Melship isn't directly involved with any of the persistent car companies. They are not providing him with any services, nor even with any, say, vacations etcetera. It isn't as blatant as some of them who 'cannot recollect' where funds or £30,000 holidays came from. And he is not doing anything towards raising funds for the party on the promise of Knighthoods, like some I could mention. By most Westminster definitions he would be squeaky-clean."

"But what about the 'industrial tourism'? " Asks Clare, "Lottie, you have accompanied him to several locations recently. Surely, he can find out about cars without visiting Wolfsburg, Munich and Tilburg."

"Agreed," says Lottie, "But all of these have been Executive Briefing Centre trips. You fly there, stay overnight in a hotel, where a couple of British representatives of the company try to get you drunk whilst telling stories about how great they are.

"Then, next day, you get bussed to their luxurious briefing centre where they offer elaborate breakfasts and then a succession of presenters who have dumbed down everything to fit into 45-minute segments."

Lottie sighed, "A couple of coffee breaks, a lunch

and a spin around a test track in a so-called secret wonder car which has been painted to look like a boulder avalanche in a snow field. Melship seems to enjoy it and often stays on for a couple of days at the end of a visit. I grab the first flight back and feel as if I've been processed like a slice of Kraft cheese."

"There must be so much to do in Wolfsburg and Tilburg?" laughs Clare.

"Actually, there was a well-known sleaze scandal attached to Wolfsburg - 'The Wolfsburg Fortress Mentality' as it was known in the German Press," answers Tessa, " You should google it for the salacious details."

"Well, now Melship is looking forward to the visit to the Motor Trade Show in Switzerland. And a couple of the car companies there are bidding for places on his table. They are targeting him, rather than the celebrity host - Jallie T."

"I suppose it is quite clever really. A form of camouflage to target the influencer under the guise of targeting the celebrity!" says Clare.

"It is surprisingly common actually," says Cat. "I get asked to go to all kinds of events with potential clients. Sometimes it is lavish restaurants, other times it is formal events like theatre and opera. Corax always seems to have a golden key to gain access for our client to anyone."

Tessa brings over a fresh bottle of chilled white

wine.

Lottie laughs, "Tessa - will you never learn!"

"So, Cat, you know about companies and shares and things?" asks Clare.

"Shop!" say Lottie and Tessa simultaneously.

"No let her go on," says Cat, "I'm intrigued."

"Well, we've been following a lead for a company called Zillian. They manufacture cars, mainly."

"Ach, yes, Zillian. A very mysterious company." Answers Cat.

"You know they make electric cars and vans?" asks Cat.

"Erm, I don't really know much about them at all. I was hoping you could help me find out some more."

"Well, it's not my area, but I know someone that trades automotive and he'll probably have the information. Are you planning to invest or something, only you seem to have a very shaky knowledge."?

Clare answers, "No, we were looking at them as part of a company profile, but there seems to be some doubts about their scale of operation." She was determined not to reveal anything about the situation with Melship and she could see Lottie give her a glance, which was like 'you'd better stop now.'

Cat answers, "Leave it with me, I'll get my man to dig into it for you. I expect we have an analyst profile piece or something."

Cat returns with information

Clare's phone rings. She is in Andrew Brading's office in Parliament. It is Cat.

"Hi, it's Cat. I've got the information you asked about, but there is quite a lot of it. Will Hanson is the analyst and he's said he'll provide a briefing for you. I told him you were something in Parliament and he couldn't wait!"

"But it might be difficult to find a briefing room. Leave it with me, and I'll get back by midday tomorrow."

Clare calls Jake.

"I can get a briefing about Zillian, the car company mixed up in the Melship briefing, but the guy concerned - Will Hanson - wants it to be linked with a trip around Parliament. Have you got any ideas?"

Jake pauses and then says, "Amanda wanted to have a catch-up briefing. Why don't I ask her if we can run it from Vauxhall Cross? That way you could meet Hanson at Parliament, but then bring him over to SI6? I could ask Amanda to lay on a car, maybe? - A little theatre thrown in?"

"Brilliant plan. Let me tell Cat about the offer. I'm sure it will work."

Right through you

Wait a minute man
You mispronounced my name
You didn't wait for all the information
Before you turned me away
Wait a minute sir
You kind of hurt my feelings
You see me as a sweet back-loaded puppet
And you've got a meal ticket taste

I see right through you
I know right through you
I feel right through you
I walk right through you

You took me for a joke
You took me for a child
You took a long hard look at my ass
And then played golf for a while
Your shake is like a fish
You pat me on the head
You took me out to wine dine 69 me
But didn't hear a damn word I said

Now that I'm Miss Thing
Now that I'm a zillionaire
You scan the credits for your name
And wonder why it's not there

Alanis Nadine Morissette / Basil Glen Ballard

Undetectable Firearms Act

Jake had made sure it was all arranged for the briefing from Will Hanson.

Clare was to meet Lottie, Cat Maier, and Will Hanson at Parliament, but then get them all ferried out in an SI6 SUV and along to Vauxhall Cross.

Clare arranged to meet them at Portcullis House. They could get visitor passes and have a coffee and then she could take the tunnel to the main Parliament buildings. It was a quick way to impress Will.

Lottie smiled when she heard Clare's plan. Amanda Miller had provisioned a couple of Range-Rovers to ferry them along to SI6 and they would be able to come out of the underground car park and out through the main gates of Parliament. Clare knew that there was a regular ferrying of people to and from Parliament and to various buildings around the immediate area.

Lottie asked Jake, "But this must be quite an important meeting if you are involving SI6 and getting us all ferried from Parly to SI6?"

"Oh yes, Amanda is most interested now she thinks we are on to something. I didn't expect to get two cars through!" says Clare.

Sure enough, Cat and Will arrived and Lottie and Clare dished some hospitality on them both. It was all routine for them, but it was impressing Will and Cat. She hadn't told Will that they were heading along the river to SI6's building.

"Time to move, " says Clare, "We're being picked up."

"Where are we going?" asks Will. He looked at Cat, but it was plain that she didn't know either.

"We have to run the briefing at SI6, which is just along the river. We are being taken there in special vehicles."

"Oh, I don't know about this," says Will, looking concerned.

"You'll be going to the building they use in all the James Bond movies," explains Lottie.

"You'll probably need to sign the Official Secrets Act as well," adds Clare.

They were walking to the underground car park

adjacent to the Big Ben clock tower. Standing by a couple of marked bays, Clare rang for the cars.

Two black Range Rovers slipped quietly into the parking spots.

"You'd better climb in and make the most of this journey," says Clare, "People will think you are a diplomat or a spy, travelling like this!"

Clare noticed that there was already someone in the front passenger seat of the first car. She didn't want to admit that it was the first time she had been transported in this manner.

Lottie wasn't as cool and says, "Clare: the friend who just keeps on giving!"

They slip out of the car park, up a short ramp, past some traffic lights and a couple of serious-looking yellow and black-painted barriers and then a couple of policemen open the gates and shoo the pedestrians away so that they can make their exit.

Clare noticed that the cars both had blue flashing lights, but no sirens as they gently made their way along the river's edge towards Vauxhall.

Then over Vauxhall Bridge and in a matter of moments they were in tunnels which led into the security services building.

They were shown out of the cars. Clare realised that both cars had a member of SI6 sitting in the front passenger seat and these two individuals showed the four of them into the building. There was a familiar routine of handing over phones and showing identities.

Clare realised it was some time since she was last in SI6, and that she had been reset to an occasional visitor status.

Then, at last, they were ready to move to a conference room. It was on a low floor and looked out of the back of the building, away from the Thames.

Amanda Miller appeared and greeted Clare.

"You must be Lottie," she asks, " Which would make you two Katherina Maier and William Hanson?"

"It's Cat, actually," says Cat and then adds, "Oh and Will!"

Amanda smiles, "We are going through to another room in a moment. Jake is in there, along with Bigsy and Christina. I thought if you were all involved, then we could cross brief one-another together."

Will looks slightly stunned by all of this. He'd only responded to a minor request from Cat and now, in one day, he had experienced more of the Secret Service than he'd ever watched in spy films.

Cat speaks to Lottie, "Yes, I am beginning to see what you meant about Clare's range of surprises!"

"Okay, before we go further, I need to know that you don't have any weapons?" asks Amanda, "Your colleague Christina was carrying a Glock 17 pistol, which we had to confiscate."

Clare notices Will's eyes go from large to almost pop from his head at this revelation. Cat breathes to Lottie, "Okay, I'll believe everything you say from now on."

Amanda led them along a short corridor. There were a couple of numbered doors on each side as well as the one into the conference facility. Clare noticed they were back on the river side of the building and considered that Amanda must be suitably senior to get these best spots.

Inside, already sitting round a table were Bigsy, Jake, and Christina as well as Grace from GCHQ, who immediately recognised Clare and came around the table to greet her.

"I didn't expect to be working together so soon!" she says smiling, "and this has some curious similarities with those other situations - Medusa and Minerva."

Clare replies, "I thought that at first, but I'm less convinced now. I think the Russians have given up on their attempts to blackmail lobbyists. I think this has the hallmark of an internally generated situation."

Amanda speaks, "Okay everyone, we'll do a quick

around the table introductions. I'll remind everyone that this meeting falls within the Official Secrets Act and that anyone disclosing anything from here can be prosecuted and may face imprisonment.

"When you came through the reception, we asked each of you to sign your MOD 134s which is a full Duty of Confidentiality"

Clare Bigsy, Jake, and Christina were all used to this protocol but Clare could see that Lottie, Cat and Will needed some time to process the information

Then Amanda asked Will about his background.

"I guess I'm just starting out, really. I thought my MBA was really table stakes for this role. Now I'm in it I can see that there are so many graduates and even 18-year-olds attempting to get into the business. It's like an episode of the Apprentice each time a fresh batch arrives.

"They said my role was a senior level position responsible for assisting clients in raising funds in the capital markets, as well as in providing strategic advisory services for mergers, acquisitions and other types of financial transactions.

Will continued, "...And I know I'm in the business, but now there's investment advice channels being run by 20-year-old video-bloggers. It has all become rather scary in a 'JFK's father' kind of way. He said, just before the 1929 stock market crash..."

Jake interrupts, "I know this one, 'If shoeshine boys are giving stock tips, then it's time to get out of the market.'"

"Yes, spot on. You must think like an economist," says Will, "If history is particular; economics is general —it involves searching for patterns which indicate if a cycle is turning. Today's financial system looks nothing like it did before the crashes of 2001 and 2008, yet lately there have been some familiar signs of froth and fear on Wall Street: wild trading days on no real news, sudden price swings and a queasy feeling among many investors that they have overdosed on techno-optimism."

"So, it is really one big casino!" says Clare.

Will continues, "To give you an example. Shares soared in 2021, then, in January 2022 Wall Street had their worst January since 2009, falling by 5.3%. The prices of assets favoured by retail investors, like tech stocks, cryptocurrencies, and shares in electric-car makers, all plunged, like some kind of Stockbroker board game. The once-giddy mood on reddit/wallstreetbets, which is a forum for digital day-traders, slumped.

Will continues, "It is tempting to think that the January sell-off was exactly what was needed, purging the stock market of its speculative excesses. But the global financial system is still loaded with risks. Asset prices are high: the last time shares were so pricey relative to long-run profits was before the slumps of 1929 and 2001, and the extra return for owning risky bonds is near its lowest level for a quarter of a century.

"Many portfolios loaded up on long-duration assets that yield profits only in the distant future. And central banks are raising interest rates to tame inflation. America's Federal Reserve is expected to making regular quarter-point increases.

"Now it would be good to say that this was all under control, but it has become a case of 'no-body knows'. It's all wrapped up in machine algorithms, which automatically micro adjust as part of high-speed trading systems. Analysts invent a new slice of logic, plug it in, and it's like an anti-missile missile chasing its prey. And just as explosive."

"Like the fibre optic shortcut that Michael Lewis described in Flash Boys? The one that cut 5 milliseconds off a high frequency trade?" asks Jake.

"Well, that was a more physical manifestation, along with the microwave towers that followed it, " says Will.

"I see it's like betting on the outcome of a horse race when you know the winner?" says Clare, "Like that Redford movie - The Sting?"

"Correct," said Will, "Although you only have milliseconds in which to accomplish all of this. But of course, the odds are loaded in favour of the Flash Boys. All of the time."

Will continued, "But if we look at the bigger forces, the mix of sky-high valuations and rising interest rates could easily result in large losses, as the rate used to discount future income rises. If big losses do materialise, the important question, for investors, for central bankers and for the world economy, is whether the financial system will safely absorb them or amplify them?"

"Are we all doomed, then?" asks Bigsy.

Will answers, "The answer is not obvious, for that system has been transformed over the past 15 years by the twin forces of regulation and technological innovation. For example, new capital rules have pushed a lot of risk-taking out of banks. At the same time, digitisation has given computers more decision-making power, created new platforms for owning assets and cut the cost of trading almost to zero."

"The result is a high-frequency, market-based system with a new cast of players. Share-trading is no longer dominated by pension funds but by automated exchange-traded funds (ETFs) and swarms of retail investors using slick new apps."

Will continues, "For example, borrowers can tap debt funds as well as banks. Credit flows across borders thanks to asset managers such as BlackRock, which buy foreign bonds, not just global lenders such as Citigroup.

These markets operate at breakneck speed: the

volume of shares traded in America is 3.8 times what it was a decade ago. Many of these changes have been for the better. They have made it cheaper and easier for all types of investors to deal in a broader range of assets.

But, like JFK's father's shoe-shine boy's ideas, the crash of 2008-09 showed how dangerous it was to have banks that took deposits from the public exposed to catastrophic losses, which forced governments to bail them out.

Today banks are less central to the financial system, better capitalised and hold fewer highly risky assets. More risk-taking is done by funds backed by shareholders or long-term savers who, on paper, are better equipped to absorb losses.

And there's the shadow players. The reinvention of finance has not eliminated hubris.

Two dangers stand out.

First, some leverage is hidden in shadow banks and investment funds. I'm talking about the equivalent of nation state funding hidden behind a clever wrapper. Russia and China spring to mind as key actors in this space, but they are using smaller players to legitimise the front ends of their dealings. Charles Abridge-Bois springs to mind.

"I always think his name sounds like a bus route," says Bigsy.

"A Victorian one? With wooden bench seats?" suggests Jake.

Will added, "Laugh all you might, he's still gaining money at a rate that would make some forgers blush. Through an off-shore company where most of it is going to the Caymans or similar places offshore."

"But I've seen him in Parliament, lounging about in the commons," says Bigsy, "He looks louche but not like a spiv."

"Appearances may deceive," infers Will, "And there's plenty with a finger in this pie."

"For example, the total borrowings and deposit-like liabilities of hedge funds, property trusts and money market funds have risen to 43% of GDP, from 32% a decade ago. Firms can rack up huge debts without anyone noticing."

"There's only a few places where this is easier than the UK, and that's where the action is evolving.

"As an example, take Singapore. Singapore is open as an international financial, investment, and transport hub which exposes it to money laundering and terrorist financing risks.

"The country's position as the most stable and prominent financial centre in Southeast Asia, coupled with a regional history of transnational organised crime, large-scale corruption in neighbouring states, and a range of other offenses in those states increase the risk that Singapore will be viewed as an attractive destination for criminals to launder their criminal proceeds.

He adds, "Limited large currency reporting requirements and the size and growth of Singapore's private banking and asset management sectors also pose inherent risks. Among the types of illicit activity noted in the region are fund flows associated with illegal activity in Australia that transit Singapore financial service providers for other parts of Asia."

Jake adds, "Yes, now that London has freed itself from EU legislation, the fat cats are eyeing Singapore as an interesting model."

Will continues, "There's around 40 offshore banks in operation, all foreign-owned. Singapore is a major centre for offshore private banking and asset management.

Assets under management in Singapore total approximately $2 trillion. As of the end of 2014, Singapore has approximately $1.5 trillion in foreign funds under management. Singapore does not permit shell banks or anonymous accounts.

Jake mused, "You don't have to be a sovereign state to be interested in the potential of London, just blend in offshore banking and some Freetrade zones and it all starts to pull together. The likes of Charles Abridge-Bois, will be licking their lips in anticipation of the new prizes on offer."

Will nods, "An example: A Chinese trader created a business in Singapore which had $10 billion under management as of 2020. His previous company had pleaded guilty to insider trading of Chinese bank stocks in 2012 and paid a $44 million fine. The holdings were primarily in the form of total return swaps, a technical financial instrument where the underlying securities (stocks) are held by banks."

Clare speaks, "Hmm, I'm a bit hazy on total return swaps!"

Will adds, "It meant that they did not need to disclose its large holdings, while if it had transacted in regular stocks, it would have had to. The fund was also heavily leveraged and did business with multiple banks which were likely unaware of the large positions held by other banks.

"Like borrowing money against the same collateral multiple times?" asks Clare.

"Exactly," says Will, "Of course, it crashed and several big and well-known banks had to take the financial hit, measured in billions of dollars. Simply put if asset prices fall, other blow-ups follow, accelerating the correction."

Will continues, "The second danger is that, although the new system is more decentralised, it still relies on transactions being channelled through a few nodes that could be overwhelmed by volatility. Exchange-traded funds, with $10 trillion of assets, rely on a few small market-making firms to ensure that the price of funds accurately tracks the underlying assets they own.

Then Will adds, for emphasis, "Trillions of dollars of derivatives contracts are routed through five American clearing houses. These transactions are executed by a new breed of middlemen, such as Citadel for hedge funds and the related Citadel Securities, for 40% of the stock trades in the USA. The Treasury market now depends on automated high-frequency trading firms to function."

"All these firms or institutions hold safety buffers and most can demand further collateral or "margin" to protect themselves from their users' losses."

Cat speaks, "Yet recent experience suggests reasons for concern. The market-based financial system is hyperactive most of the time; in times of stress whole areas of trading activity can dry up. That can fuel panic."

Will speaks again, "Exactly, Cat. Ordinary citizens may not think it matters much if a bunch of day-traders and fund managers get burned. But such a fire could damage the rest of the economy. Fully 53% of American households own shares (up from 37% in 1992), and there are over 100m online brokerage accounts. And of course, it all feeds through into pension plans."

Cat speaks again, "If credit markets gum up, households and firms will struggle to borrow. That is why, at the start of the pandemic, the Fed acted as a "market-maker of last resort," promising up to $3 trillion to support a range of debt markets and to backstop dealers and some mutual funds."

"Maximum score," thought Clare.

Will continues, "In reality, I spend most of my time producing reports like the one I gave to Cat.

"I guess that means your report is quite balanced, then?" asks Amanda.

"I hope so; although this one won't have been re-edited by a Chief Analyst to hit the investment criteria, we need to Value Sell the proposition," answered Will.

Cat smiles, "We both sound like buzz-word compliant corporates, because it's what we do all day!"

Clare and Jake both laugh, and Will continues, "Cat has never asked me for anything before, and I had no idea she related to such people as yourselves. You all seem to be spies or something? I mean one of you was even carrying a weapon."

Christina replies, "Well it was concealed and being made of polymer I didn't think the scanners would see it."

Amanda answers, "We've had plenty of time since the Undetectable Firearms Act of 1983 to perfect better scanning. But Will, you should tell us what you have discovered?"

Will starts to speak, "If you want to gauge the market's feelings towards the future of sustainable mobility, look no further than electric vehicle maker Zillian."

"The company is predicted to have an opening market value greater than Ford or General Motors."

Will looks baffled, "What makes this strange is that it doesn't have any product yet. So far it has produced a total of around a dozen vehicles, half of which were vans.

"Last quarter, it only generated around £2 million in revenue. That's not profits. It's total revenue. Now it isn't the only disruptive new company in the automotive space. There's been that well-known electric car manufacturer which sent one of its cars into space for publicity. And there's at least a couple of other fledgling start-ups.

Christina speaks, "I guess we could say 'powered by twitter' features strong and the Millennial generation of investors."

"And there's something else," adds Will, "The Zillian prospectus looks kinda hokey."

"Technical phrase!" interjects Cat.

Will continues, looking serious, "The thing is, when

I went along to their own corporate website, the bumpf looked suspect. It looked as if it had been lifted from somewhere else by an undergraduate trainee.

"To be honest, I thought it was text from a software company. Nothing about engines, driving experience, comfort etc. All about management, as if it was a systems software purveyor."

"A couple of examples," Will looks at a small notebook.

"Our proprietary management platform helps optimize and automate fleet operations to help improve your total cost of ownership and maximize uptime.

"Cloud-based tools conveniently accessible on multiple devices."

"Our team of experts work with you from initial planning to installation providing a full turnkey site deployment solution"

Bigsy interrupts, "It sounds more like server systems management solution than a car firm,"

"Yes, that's what I was thinking. You could almost edit in the 'car specific' words. Another example, 'Engineered specifically for fleets to help you achieve an exceptional total cost of ownership.'

"Paper Tiger?" Asks Grace,

"Wow, I haven't heard that in a long time," replies Amanda.

Grace adds, "Mao Zedong was keen to use the phrase - 'In appearance it is very powerful but, it is nothing to be afraid of; it is a paper tiger. Outwardly a tiger but made of paper, unable to withstand the wind and the rain.'"

"That was American Imperialism, I think?" says Cat.

"Ah, so you are breaking cover as a historian?" asks Amanda.

"PPE at Uni," says Cat, "Don't ask me how I ended up doing banking!"

"So, what do we think?" says Jake. He looked toward Amanda's analyst Grace.

Grace says, "Yes, I agree with Will's analysis, but we need to think why, ask a few 'and then what?' type questions."

Christina suggests, "Maybe someone is starting a new money laundry? This could be huge in scale. It would need some state backing to be able to start it up. I could see the Kremlin making a play like this."

Grace speaks again, "Yes, if someone is thinking of how to fire up a semi-state type enterprise, then this would be a way to raise funds."

Will looks at them both, "You are thinking about this as if it would be used illegally. There's all kinds of legislation around to prevent those kinds of things."

"Just like the no-plastic guns legislation?" says Amanda.

"Exactly," says Grace, I can show you several sites where the software instructions to print plastic guns are stored. To be honest, plastics are being superseded by CNC-milling operations nowadays. Take a block of metal and machine it to make an untraceable semi-automatic. A ghost gun."

"Jake chimes in, "Rules: For the obedience of fools and guidance of wise?"

"More like 'proceed until apprehended,' "says Clare

"But the sheer scale of a company share floatation?" asks Will.

"Precisely, its what's called 'hiding in plain sight,' " says Amanda.

"Okay, what else do we know?" asks Amanda.

Lottie speaks, "There is some sad news. Isabella Stevens, who worked for Douglas Lessiter, was found in the Thames this morning. She was spotted by one of the commuter boats. It's in the papers now." She opened her phone and displayed a front page from one of the London news feeds.

"My god!" says Clare, looking startled, "it's the woman that was with Lessiter at the Xmas party. I didn't know her, but I got involved in rescuing her from a difficult situation during the party. There was some kind of an argument."

Lottie looks over, slightly shocked, "Yes, I know Hannah from Lessiter's office. I'd seen the two of them around together. I'm sure Hannah is shaken up by this, but I'll see if there is any other news."

Grace looks at her laptop and reads, "Early statements suggest that there was no foul play and it looked like tragic accident. She appeared to have a high Blood Alcohol Content level of 0.35."

"0.35 is enough to induce a coma," says Amanda, "It is an unrealistically high amount to get from an office party, unless the drink was massively spiked."

"There will be big attempts to decouple this from a government office party," says Clare, "Brace yourselves!"

Lottie speaks, "Back to Melship. Since he has been Secretary of State for the Department for Transport Efficiency, he has been inundated with requests from every car manufacturer. They all want to wine and dine him, then spring some influence. They play him like a fool. The ultimate sweet back-loaded puppet."

Clare laughs, then Jake says, "I'm not quite sure what that means."

Grace says, "There's nothing else out of the ordinary about Zillian, that I could spot. It looks just like generic corporation positioning for a floatation."

Will nods, "Exactly. It looks almost too generic. Where's it's unique selling points that all make the market want to buy it?"

"Where are its existing products?" Adds Grace, "The Emperor has no clothes."

"We'll find out soon enough," says Jake, "The Geneva Car Expo approaches."

Kotyonok

Saturday at Heathrow Airport and Clare waited for the plane with Christina and her 'table group'. Douglas Melship had gone through to the business lounge with Lottie.

Christina Nott was with her car show 'second table' treating the whole trip as if it was part of a road tour. Jake and Bigsy accompanied her, with Jake as a surrogate Road Manager and Bigsy as technical support.

They had taken a small corner of the lounge and were keeping themselves to themselves when a stranger appeared and motioned Christina to one side.

"My god!" uttered Christina in amazement, "I didn't expect to see you here!"

A leather-jacketed man strode towards her. He had a military haircut and grabbed Christina in both arms.

"Ha, kotyonok, what mischief are you in this time?"

It was Antanov Chekeryn, who Christina originally knew from the Academy in Arkangelsk. They had worked together a few times and she knew that Antanov was entirely dependable.

"Kotyonok - kitten! - But you. You bring memories of good times on helicopters! I guess this has something to do with Blackbird?"

Blackbird was Fyodor Kuznetsov, her handler. Although she had always thought that Kuznetsov's code name was just a little too close to 'blacksmith', which was the English translation of Kuznetsov.

"Yes, " smiled Antonov, "After you reported back to Blackbird about this suspected attempt at lobbying, Blackbird was asked to intervene. Because your operational style is somewhat unusual, zvezda moya, he asked me to also take a look."

"Usually, The Kremlin is all over these situations," said Christina, "Not this time," replied Antonov, "In fact Blackbird wondered if it was something from China."

"Okay, so that also rules out Russian organised crime," said Christina, "and the United States. This could be a wholly new operative?"

Antanov replied, "Well, I'm going to Geneva as part of the Radiant Tyre Company. Radiant produce 20% of the radial tyres in Russia, apparently. I'll be checking up on things while I'm there. I wanted to let you know so that we can stay in touch whilst you are there."

"You know what, you are still in my cellphone, " said Christina and to prove it rang the number. Sure enough Antanov's phone rang."

He held it up so that she could read the name. 'Kotyonok', it displayed - Kitten.

"Okay, well I guess you know we are also going to Gstaad as part of the VIP Programme?" asked Christina.

"Yes, me too. Although I'm borrowing a helicopter to get there. I'll fly myself from Geneva. And you never know when a helicopter becomes a useful field asset."

Christina smiled. Antanov was still a man of action.

Geneva

As they landed in Geneva, Clare could see snow and various types of de-icing system being deployed on planes getting ready for take-off.

Then, through Arrivals and onward to the bag check.

There were many delegates queuing at the various luggage belts. Clare, Christina, Jake and Bigsy decided to share a taxi to the hotel. Most of them had 'Bus Line A' tickets from the organisers except Christina's preferential 'Bus Line B'.

Sure enough, Bus Line A's queue stretched a long way from outside and back into the terminal building.

Bigsy hailed a large VW taxi, which was some kind of minibus and they loaded their luggage on board and then sat in tidy rows of seats. "It's like a mini-road tour!" said Clare and Christina laughed.

Then Clare noticed from the corner of her eye the signs for Bus Line B. It led to a taxi rank, except instead of taxis, there were high-end saloon cars to whisk the privileged to their hotels. She noticed Melship and Lottie waiting in the line but decided not to wave.

Their taxi driver was polite, but slightly bemused that the group wanted to be driven to the hotel.

"It is only a few minutes' walk from the airport and from the Palexpo.", he explained. But they asked him to drive them anyway, and Bigsy made sure he received a good tip.

"The advantage of this hotel is that it is right by the Expo and the airport yet is only around 15 minutes to get into the centre of Geneva'" explained Bigsy, who had made the detailed logistical arrangements.

The driver added, "It is quite clever of the organisers because many visitors will stay around here, and the main thing to do is visit the show, rather than getting a diffusion of visitors into Geneva. Most people will go into the city maybe once, or twice, but mainly they will be immersed in the car industry and all of its charms."

Sure enough, the hotel had various prestige cars parked outside and inside there were a couple of brightly coloured exotic-looking sports cars raised into the air.

As they checked in, Clare noticed a row of

hospitality desks, arranged by various well - known car companies. It was clear that many guests were to be pampered at this event. No wonder Duncan Melship was so eager to attend.

Then, at check-in, they were each handed a bag of complementary products. Clare expected it to be brake fluid or anti-freeze, but it turned out to be expensive perfume from France and delicious-looking chocolates from Switzerland.

Christina was given a larger bag as well, which contained a sleek red leather backpack by Wenger - a Swiss manufacturer.

They were all given registration instructions. As well as checking into the hotel, they needed to check in for the event.

"You've hit the jackpot," said Jake, smiling as Christina and Clare cooed over the bag.

Then they noticed Melship and Lottie arrive. They were with Douglas Lessiter and his assistant Hannah. Duncan Melship was looking harassed. Lottie smiled to them but her expression indicated they should stay away.

Melship was saying, "How could they lose my bag so quickly? I mean it was a short flight from London and yet my bag with all my briefing papers for the conference has gone missing."

They could hear Lottie speaking, " The organisers

have a 'perte de bagages' room. I'm sure yours will turn up there. In the meantime, I have everything on my laptop. But I think we'll need to be ready for tonight's meeting with Express Fleet Management. I think the reception for it starts in about an hour."

Jake realised what was happening. "They must have filled Melship's itinerary. It's a common trick to swamp the target with receptions, meeting, and meals. Almost like sensory overload. He'll be flagging by time he is scheduled to visit Gstaad."

"Yes, but I think his disappearing baggage might be something else," said Christina. "Someone wants to see or get inside it."

"What? Read what is in it, or bug it?" asked Jake.

"That's my theory," said Christina, "and it is not a very subtle attempt."

"Does that mean you are suspicious of your shiny new luggage?" asked Jake.

"Not really, look around. There's already a handful of others with the bags - even Lottie, look!"

"She must have been on the same kind of privileged ticket as Melship," said Clare.

"Just a moment," said Christina. She walked back to the registration desk and talked for a few minutes to the person controlling it. Then she returned.

"Clare, go back to the desk, see that man on the left-hand end position. Say you are my personal assistant."

Clare did as she was asked and to her surprise, the man presented her with the larger complementary bag. Clare could not believe her luck. "Oh yes, and we have these for assistants too," he looked behind him and produced a small white box containing an iPod Touch. "It's been preloaded with the itinerary and you can use it to select the sessions for Ms Nott."

Clare happily received this electronic goody and returned to the others.

"It's a bit embarrassing, I've now got one of those excellent bags, which has the same perfume and other things in it as my original one, plus a complementary iPod to help us get around the show!"

"Did you see the piles of those bags behind the registration desk?" asked Jake, "They must be immune to the value they are handing out!"

"And it shows how much this industry is awash with marketing budget!" added Bigsy.

Clare's' phone pinged. It was a message from Lottie.

"Busy tonight, will see you for breakfast tomorrow. 8am."

"Lottie is busy with Melship's itinerary; I guess at

least we have someone on the inside," said Clare.

"Like us; we need to be on the inside of a bar right now, " said Jake, "Let's get to our rooms and meet up in, say, half an hour. We can go to that bar over there."

Breakfast

Next morning, they assembled for breakfast.

"The discussion yesterday evening was entirely out of my comfort zone," says Clare, "Those guys in the bar, the salesmen, were so sure of themselves and they all seemed to be running on unlimited expenses."

Jake nods and says, "It was an interesting dilemma, for them. They could see two attractive women sitting with us but were torn when they felt that there was a fleet buyer around or someone important from a government."

Clare smiles, "Christina or a fleet buyer. Honestly!"

Jake smiles also, "Yes, no contest. Christina and Clare, every time."

Clare playfully elbows Jake in the ribs, "But seriously, do you think you can continue to talk about cars for a whole week?"

She adds, "Wheels. Tyres. Doors. Engines. Litres per 100km. Sunroofs. Satnav. Electricity. Environmental impact."

"Something I learnt is that most of the new electric cars look like my old toy car racing set," says Bigsy, "One chassis can take many car bodies."

"Yes, and the chassis is entirely made of little batteries," adds Jake.

Clare speaks, "I guess the whole automotive industry will have to find new things to talk about. Open the bonnet, it's empty! Luggage space. Open the boot, it's also empty! More luggage space. No dials since they made the dashboard look like a smartphone. Then the two or three electric motors on each of the axles. They don't even make a noise. It's not like talking about a 3-litre V6 or a V12. What will men in pubs discuss?"

Jake replies, "That's easy... I drove silently all the way from London to Hull and only had to stop once for a very long coffee break whilst I recharged. I took plenty of luggage with me because of all the storage space."

"Maybe that's why they were giving away free bags to Christina and Clare yesterday?" adds Bigsy, "encouraging greater luggage use?"

Lottie arrives. She looks harassed. "Melship was at a meeting last night with the people from a fleet management company. I thought this was an almost missable meeting, but it turns out they want to do something like the bikes in London and have a lot of hire-cars on street corners. It's a taste of things to come."

"What was Melship's attitude?"

Lottie explains, "Well he had been placed next to a gorgeous blonde who seemed to be explaining what the various 'key points' from the discussion were about. Melship was caught in her headlights, so to speak, and didn't really know what to say."

She continues, "They were asking for his agreement in principle to support a new kind of charger. It was proprietary, so it would only work with their hire cars. It all sounded like a nightmare to me."

Bigsy says, "I see what they are doing. Trying to sew up London's streets with their own private design of vehicle. It's like a land grab."

"Have you been into the main hall yet?" asks Lottie. Everyone shook their heads.

"It is immense and full of cars. I say full, but there is quite a lot of room to walk around the vehicles and even climb in them. There's also a whole range of smart-suited salesmen and a few women out there. I thought the sexist battle about car marketing had been fought, but there still seem to be a lot of lightly clad bodies draped over bonnets."

"We used to call them 'booth babes' and 'grid girls' for the Formula One, when I worked for Street," says Jake, "And I'm pretty sure that exhibitors are still free to choose how they want to present their vehicles."

Jake continues, "I dated a model who used to work for car companies. She told me they had secret signals, such as tucking hair behind their ears, when they wanted help in fending off overly eager patrons.

"And some of the car companies said it makes more sense to use product specialists who knew about the cars."

Bigsy adds, "It's like those silly giveaways - they also do it at tech shows. Some show visitors grab a big bag and then try to fill it up with all the freebies on offer. What use is it if you manage to capture their business card. Are they a serious buyer? I think not."

Clare speaks, "I guess #METOO has had some impact then? On this most exploitative of industries."

Jake, "Yes but it will take a long time to work its way into an industry that top to bottom has glamour calendars - even for car tyres."

Bigsy adds, "And think about the lack of interesting things to talk about with new cars: '...It's battery operated!' "

Clare asks, "So, did we learn anything new?"

"Only that Duncan Melship is a liability," answers Jake.

Rinse and repeat every breakfast

Clare, Christina, Jake, Lottie and Bigsy had agreed to meet at 08:00 each morning to compare notes. It was an hour ahead of when Melship would appear and gave Lottie a chance to get some input from the rest of them.

The next morning, they met.

Clare was just saying, "In that old song it goes something like ' cars don't talk back.' - Well guess what, they do now. I didn't want my car to keep reminding about closing the doors and putting on the handbrake - and so many variations of bing bong noises."

"I'm with you on that," says Bigsy, "Although most of the newest cars have automatic handbrakes now."

Lottie laughs, "I think this was supposed to help Duncan, but I think it might be confusing him."

At that moment, Hannah appears, "Hi guys, I

thought I saw you here yesterday morning. Clever to get in to breakfast before our esteemed bosses."

"How are you?" asks Lottie. She looks concerned, "It must have been quite a shock when Isabella disappeared like that? Our condolences."

Hannah looks toward the group eating their croissants and Swiss cheese.

"I'm not convinced about that whole situation," she whispers, "Look, I don't know all of you sitting here, so maybe I shouldn't say more..."

Lottie replies, "Hannah, you remember Clare, from Andrew Brading's office? And these other people are my trusted friends. Jake, Bigsy and Christina. They all have the highest clearances, one could say, right through to Vauxhall Cross."

"Oh, you are agents?" asks Hannah, "And Lottie is vouching for you, so I'd just remind you about secrecy if I carry on explaining."

Jake, Bigsy and Christina all looked suitably sombre and Jake says, "Yes we heard about your colleague."

"I was there, at the party, when Isabella was last seen," says Clare, "As a matter of fact I was helping her to get a taxi home. Andrew Brading and Maggie Shannon were there too and we saw events unfolding before Isabella asked me to help her leave the event."

"Did Izzy seem at all drunk to you?" asks Hannah.

"Not especially. I mean we'd all had a few drinks by that time."

"But not enough to push into chronic intoxication. The kind that could induce a coma?" asks Hannah.

"No, I didn't recognise Isabella, nor did I know her name," answers Clare, "But she seemed quite capable of lucid conversation and could walk herself to the exit."

"So, what were you doing with her?" asks Hannah, looking intrigued, "I mean, if that isn't too personal a question."

"No, no," says Clare, "As a matter of fact, I was rescuing her from an altercation with Duggie! - Maggie and I were both helping her out. She seemed to be in an intense argument with Duggie. It seemed to be more than his usual wandering hands. We could hear her saying something about an NDA."

Hannah thinks for a moment, "Oh yes, I think I know what that was about. A company that Duggie has a tie-in with. He asked us all to sign Non-Disclosure Agreements before they came to present something they were working on to us."

Clare continues, "Well, Duggie had been holding her, I'd say hard enough to bruise her skin. When Maggie and I approached, she broke away and shortly after that asked me if I would accompany her to the exit."

"I escorted her outside, and conveniently a black cab approached us and she hailed it and headed for home."

"I wonder if the entrance had any form of CCTV?" asks Hannah.

'I imagine so if that evening's comings and goings were in any way normal," says Clare.

Hannah's phone buzzes and she says, " I must run, I'm being summoned to Douglas Lessiter."

Christina speaks, "The cab. It could have been a fake. Used to pick up Isabella without raising suspicions."

Jake speaks, "I think we should handle this via Amanda, rather than getting the local police involved. I'll call her when we finish breakfast."

"Okay - We'll see you later at the 'Battery Presentation,' says Clare. Bigsy laughs.

Range anxiety

Clare, Christina, Bigsy, Lottie and Jake trooped their way to a main Ballroom area, which was a floor higher than the main Expo. Sure enough, inside the vast ballroom were many seats - mainly occupied - with large screen repeaters either side of a brightly lit stage. They sat near to the back, well out of direct earshot of the presenters.

Then, Saul Chadnitz walked onto the stage to 'The Power' by Snap, followed by Angela Rolls. They were both in white tee shirts and blue jeans, like a corporate dress-down code.

"Industrial Theatre," breathed Bigsy, and the others agreed.

Angela Rolls opened the session:

"Evangelist, luminary, writer, presenter, marketeer, teacher. Saul has spent most of his professional life on hot relevant topics.

"Saul is the publisher of around 20 best-selling books and I'm sure most of this audience have read at least one."

"Lately, Saul has been working around the area of autonomous vehicles and today's topic is batteries."

Chadnitz stood and paced across the stage.

He spoke, "Hmm, there's a lot of you here. I wonder how many are really interested in batteries? I know, let's do a show of hands."

"He's using voice boosting software," murmurs Bigsy, "Compression and subtle reverb."

Yet no one put their hand up to his request for a show of hands.

"Not yet. I haven't asked the question yet.

"Here we go. How many you are anxious today right now? Show of hands?"

He looked around.

"What? Nobody? I can't believe that, Ah Sir, you there - thank you for being honest."

"Well, look at the numbers... only maybe 5% of this hall is anxious right now.

Undaunted, he continued, "Now another question. If you'd come here by electric vehicle and knew you needed to get back to, say, Paris, but you had parked without a recharge, then who would be anxious?"

"More of you, maybe half."

"Now let's say you had to get back to, say, London. It's around 1000km." Would any more of you put up your hands. Maybe that's three quarters of the people in the ballroom."

He studies the hall, "And we have a name for it...Range Anxiety."

"Invented by a man," says Lottie to Clare. They both giggle.

"How come no Melship today?" whispers Clare to Lottie.

"Oh, he's off doing something with Lessiter. They are being give a special briefing about a new company. They have been asked to restrict numbers. It's all very hush-hush. Actually, I think Hannah is going along with Lessiter."

Christina says, "We should find out what they have been doing."

Chadnitz continues, "First time EV buyers are often worried about range anxiety - that feeling of being caught short on flat batteries miles from a charging point."

Christina whispers again, "Ideally we should know

who they are meeting, then we can run some background checks."

Chadnitz keeps talking, "Yet also of concern is the actual life of the battery pack. Experience with mobile phones, tablets and laptop computers has taught consumers that, over time, the batteries powering them can lose efficiency, resulting in the need for more frequent charging.

He looks around the packed hall, "So should you be worried?

"This is good marketing," whispers Clare "Educate the punters and at the same time terrify them. They will be wanting these new batteries or whatever it is Saul is about to offer."

Chadnitz continues, "Well the good news is EV cells are more resilient than you'd think, plus there are ways to make sure your car's batteries will survive better than most."

He adds, "And another thing is just how long will those batteries last?"

"Oh no!" says Clare with her arm wrapped onto her forehead, "Now I've got range anxiety but I've also got to worry about battery life!"

Chadnitz continues, "After range anxiety, battery life is one of the most common concerns for people making the jump from internal combustion-engined cars to EVs. All batteries degrade over time and with use, meaning they become less efficient as they age and, ultimately, the range of your car is reduced."

"Will the batteries still go the distance!" asks Lottie.

Clare smirks.

Chadnitz adds, "Furthermore, battery technology doesn't come cheap, and by the time the cells are in need of replacement they will cost far more to buy than the car will likely be worth - which is why we tend to replace mobile phones in their entirety rather than replace the battery pack."

Clare whispers, "I buy the car, which costs more, use the batteries, which don't go as far as advertised, so my longer journeys take even longer and after a few years the whole car is worn out because the batteries are such an expensive part." Lottie giggled.

Chadnitz continues, "Yet it's not all bad news, because there are ways to increase the lifespan of your car's battery, keeping it healthier and more efficient for longer. More importantly, while performance may degrade over time, ultimately the cells should still be providing at least 70 percent of their capacity even after 200,000 miles."

Bigsy plays with his phone, "Say a manufacturer says 260 miles range. Maybe it's a 10% exaggeration, then only top up the battery to 80%, but it degrades by 10% per year. Let's see now:

"Assume the manufacturer quotes 260 miles range.

$260*.9*.8*.9 = 168$ miles. So, I could get 100 miles less after the first year and $260*.9*.8*.7 = 131$ miles after three years. About half the original quote. Allegedly."

The others all pull faces. "Well, it's only a rough calculation," said Bigsy, "But I'm not seeing it from any of the manufacturers."

Chadnitz continues, "As an example, a number of e-taxis operating from a London airport racked up over 300,000 miles each over three years, with all retaining at least 82 percent of their charge."

Then he adds, "Perhaps the biggest single contributor to the decline in efficiency is the cycle of use and charging. Frequent draining of the cells followed by a full charge can, over time, damage the battery's ability to maintain its optimum energy storage - it's why manufacturer's typically recommend charging only to 80 percent and never letting the range drop to zero miles."

Clare whispers, "Oh no! I've got to worry about over-filling the batteries as well - Maybe there will still be things to talk about with new-style electric cars!"

Then Chadnitz picks up something from behind the podium. "This is a new type of battery. This battery features graphene, a sheet of carbon atoms bound together in a honeycomb lattice pattern."

"It looks like a regular battery to me," says Jake.

Chadnitz continues, "Let me introduce Dr. Jerrit Petrozewitz, from PowerLite Associates, based in Israel and The Netherlands. They are co-developing this new form of battery with several car companies.

Petrozewitz steps forward. "Good afternoon, everyone. Yes, it is me standing between you and lunch, but I'll hope you have something interesting to think about over your buffet selection."

"Graphene is recognized as a wonder material due to the myriad of astonishing attributes it holds. It is a potent conductor of electrical and thermal energy, extremely lightweight chemically inert, and flexible with a large surface area.

"I imagine some of you are thinking that this battery looks no different to any other but let me assure you it is. A graphene battery is light, durable, and suitable for high-capacity energy storage, as well as shortened charging times.

"Graphene will extend the battery's life, which is negatively linked to the amount of carbon that is coated on the material or added to electrodes to achieve conductivity, and graphene adds conductivity without requiring the amounts of carbon that are used in conventional batteries.

Petrozewitz adds, "Graphene can improve such battery attributes as energy density and form in various ways. Li-ion batteries can be enhanced by introducing graphene to the battery's anode and capitalising on the material's conductivity and large surface area traits to achieve morphological optimisation and performance."

"We are being evangelised to now," says Jake, "BTWBS - Baffle them with bull-shit!"

Petrozewitz adds, "It has also been discovered that creating hybrid materials can be useful for achieving battery enhancement. A hybrid of Vanadium Oxide (VO2) and graphene, for example, can be used on Li-ion cathodes and grant quick charge and discharge as well as large charge cycle durability.

Lottie whispers, "Yikes, this has turned into a science lecture. I thought VO5 was a styling gel?"

Petrozewitz contines, "In this case, VO2 offers high energy capacity but poor electrical conductivity, which can be solved by using graphene as a sort of a structural "backbone" on which to attach VO2 - creating a hybrid material that has both heightened capacity and excellent conductivity."

Then Petrozewitz reaches down and brought out another battery.

"I'm inwardly groaning," says Clare, "I'm not sure that I can take many more batteries."

Petrozewitz continues, "Another example is LFP (Lithium Iron Phosphate) batteries, that is a kind of rechargeable Li-ion battery. It has a lower energy density than other Li-ion batteries but a higher power density. Enhancing LFP cathodes with graphene allowed the batteries to be lightweight, charge much faster than Li-ion batteries and have a greater capacity than conventional LFP batteries."

"So, he's telling us that battery technology still has a way to go!" summarises Jake, "And there's some new wonder substances to make it all work."

"So, roll on the battery breakthroughs, " says Clare.

"Roll on lunch," says Bigsy.

The Raft

"This is so well organised, " says Bigsy, "I'm impressed that with our badges we can just roll into the restaurant and get marvellous food."

"You should see what they lay on for assistants!" says Lottie, "Shorter queues and waitress instead of self service."

"It's like Parliament; you just have to have the right badge!" observes Clare.

They grab a table and Hannah comes over to join them, "Hey, Hannah, you look as if your session was as dire as our one - about batteries!"

Hannah answers, "Not really, but it I'm not sure how pally Duggie and Duncan Melship are getting with a certain company. It's teetering on the edge of sleazy if you ask me!"

"Come on, you'll have to tell us. We can put you right," says Lottie, "I'm sure Duncan will spill the beans as soon as I see him, anyway."

"Well, it was all somewhat strange. It was mixed meeting. We were with Zillian and a CGI computer company - you know - the sort that makes animated space craft for use in the movies. It turns out they have something called the Raft, which is a car that runs on electric motors. Then it has cameras all over it and reference points for animators. They can drive it around and then paint onto it any computer-generated body they like. So, it could be a sports car in one shot and then an SUV in the next."

"Is that legal?" asks Bigsy, "I mean making adverts without the real car even present?"

"Apparently. It used to be more expensive than having the actual cars on location, but when some of the cars are hard to source or even still in prototype, then the Raft makes sense."

"Or so goes the marketing spiel!" says Clare.

Hannah nods, "I agree it is good to be sceptical, but my issue is putting this together with a few other things we've been briefed about. To be honest, I wondered if it is something that Isabella knew about!"

"So, what is your thinking? " Asks Christina.

"I'm wondering if the car company is trying to hype their product," answers Hannah. "Suppose they don't have anything to present? I mean, that would reduce their public perception and share price somewhat!"

"I'm not so sure," answers Bigsy, "When I went onto the show floor earlier, there were three brightly coloured Zillians on display: Yellow, Red and Blue. I agree they had been rolled into position in the hall, but I think they are being made available for test-drives to certain reviewers later in the week."

"Okay, so how can we get closer to Zillian?" asks Christina, "To try to work out if some kind of number is being played on Melship and Lessiter."

"We've got the two tables at the Gstaad event," says Clare," I seem to remember that Zillian bid to be on Melship's table, with Jallie T."

"Well, I'm looking forward to the trip to Gstaad in a supercar, tomorrow afternoon " says Jake. "After all of this hanging around being well- fed and briefed about batteries and eco-friendly non-dusty brake pads here in Geneva, we need some light relief."

The others nodded agreement, "I just hope the drivers are not going to want to talk to us about batteries," says Jake.

"Fireworks over the lake tonight, and Jallie T's band are playing close to the fountain," says Bigsy.

"Yes, she's asked me to join her for one number," says Christina, smiling.

"Not that Nirvana thing you two do?" asks Bigsy, "I suppose you'll want Clare on stage too!"

Lottie and Hannah looked intrigued.

"See, I told you, "Says Lottie to Hannah.

Firework Nirvana

Evening by the lake. Everyone had been bussed to the waterfront and it was busy with many dark-suited men in starched shirts with bow ties and women in long dresses.

Clare, Hannah, Lottie, and Christina decided to style it out with black leather jackets and dark outfits. Christina had added a red with black tartan mini-skirt, gold chains and sunglasses.

Clare was wearing her black outfit, when Cristina says, "You'll need these," and produced a pair of black round sunglasses and a small, black-rimmed hat.

"Very cool," says Lottie, and Christina looked in her bag and produced a purple bandana which she handed to Lottie and then says to Hannah, "Come with me, I've an idea!"

Ten minutes later they return and Hannah was now resplendent with faded green hair and a couple of chains.

"Sub-zero!" says Jake as he appeared with Bigsy. By comparison, they were very conservatively dressed in jeans and tee-shirts but with big coats for the bracing Geneva air.

"Christina loaned me this wig," says Hannah.

"Erm, what will Lessiter say?" asks Bigsy.

"Excellent, " says Christina ignoring the banter, "now we look like this, we should get some AAA Badges."

"AAA?" asks Hannah.

"Access All Areas, silly," says Clare.

"Clare you are still doing it," says Lottie.

Christina is already at the barrier to the stage.

"Yes, I'm Christina Nott and these are my three backing singers!" she explains. At that moment someone turned around and it was Jallie T.

"Jallie!" calls Christina.

"Make way for pop royalty!" says Jallie and the two of them hugged.

"It's been too long! And now you come equipped with three backing singers. Very cool. Hi, I'm Jallie -

I'll introduce you to my band when I can find them."

Lottie, Hannah, and Clare appear with their newly acquired wristbands - white rubber with the red AAA embossed on each of them.

"We've left lanyard territory now, moving to the next level!" says Clare.

They all laugh and Jallie goes over to greet Clare just as Rishi appeared.

"My god, great to see you, Clare!" They hug, and then Rishi notices Christina, "Babe, you are looking hot!" he says and kisses her firmly on the cheek.

"And who are your friends?" he asks, noticing Lottie and Hannah. "I suppose they are in some kind of adventure with you and it's on a need-to-know basis!" He laughs.

They all introduced themselves, then Rishi says, "And you know what? Those mallets became so popular that I order them for every venue now!"

Christina laughed and thought back to when they had first met and Rishi had persuaded Clare to take neon pink and black mallets on tour as part of a promotional pack, when they toured together with a band called Erebus. Rishi spoke into a handset and within a few moments, a small brown box containing four of the mallets had arrived.

Lottie speaks to Hannah, "See, Clare is the friend

who just keeps on giving surprises!"

Then, suddenly, Jallie T is whisked away towards a floating stage set upon Lac Leman.

"C'mon, Christina," she calls," We'll work out your spot when we are on stage."

A few minutes later, the Jallie T Band struck up their first number and the whole of the shoreline was rocking. Rishi had rigged up a monstrous light show, which Clare assumed he had borrowed from somewhere. And the PA System sounded loud enough to drown an alien invasion.

Clare, Lottie, and Hannah were all in the wings with Christina, when the band went into an extended instrumental section.

"Okay, next song!" says Jallie - "we'll do Teenage Spirit. Rishi has found us some pom-poms."

"Thank god I've been doing some gigging," said Christina, as she strode onto the stage, over a drum beat like a section from 'We will Rock You.' Boom-Boom-Clap. Boom-Booop-Clap.

"And now - for one night only - Pour un soir seulement! - Jallie T is joined on stage by Christina Nott ! - Jallie T est rejointe sur scène par Christina Nott !"

Then, a rattly guitar plays a few chords. E-A-G-C and a pounding drum bursts into the music.

Jallie T sings, on a simmer setting

"Load up on guns
  Bring your friends
  It's fun to lose
  And to pretend
  She's o-ver-bored
  Self-assured
  Oh no, I know a dirty word

By the edge of the stage, Rishi prepares a sweeping broom.

  Pom-poms edge their way to the stage.

Hello, hello, hello, how low
  Hello, hello, hello, how low
  Hello, hello, hello, how low
  Hello, hello, hello

Then a guitar slashed through the evening and the next verse, with Christina singing, carves across the stage. Jallie gestures to Lottie and Hannah, to wave the pom-poms around and they both cautiously make their way on-stage.

"Go Large!" shouts Rishi and imitates how they should push and wave the pom-poms around.

With the lights out
  It's less dangerous
  Here we are now
  Entertain us

I feel stupid
And contagious
Here we are now
Entertain us

A mulatto
An albino
A mosquito
My libido
Yeah

Clare could feel droplets of sweat running down her back from her leather jacket. How could Christina and Jallie do it? But it was exciting!

Jallie was singing again.

I'm worse at what I do best
And for this gift I feel blessed
Our little group has always been
And always will until the end

It was surprisingly difficult to keep energetically shaking a pom-pom, but the audience seemed to like it.

Hello, hello, hello, how low
Hello, hello, hello, how low
Hello, hello, hello, how low
Hello, hello, hello

Then, Jallie and Christina together.

With the lights out

It's less dangerous
Here we are now
Entertain us
I feel stupid

And contagious
Here we are now
Entertain us
A mulatto

An albino
A mosquito
My libido
Yeah

Rishi worked it with the floor broom, like in the original Nirvana video. The video that has been watched over 1.3 billion times on Youtube.

Christina again:

And I forget just why I taste
Oh yeah, I guess it makes me smile
I found it hard, it's hard to find
Oh well, whatever, nevermind

Jallie T and Christina together:

Hello, hello, hello, how low
Hello, hello, hello, how low
Hello, hello, hello, how low
Hello, hello, hello

Christina:

With the lights out
  It's less dangerous
  Here we are now
  Entertain us

They were singing alternative verses now, so Jallie took over:

I feel stupid
And contagious
Here we are now
Entertain us

Christina:

A mulatto
  An albino
  A mosquito
  My libido

Then the whole band for the last section:

A denial, a denial
  A denial, a denial
  A denial, a denial
  A denial, a denial
  A denial

Then, with a flourish, the guitar picked out the first line of 'Baby, you can drive my car' and at the end of it, Christina and Jallie sang 'Beep-beep; beep-beep - yeah!'

As the echoes of the last power chord ebb away, it merges with a crashing wave of applause from the audience. They were going wild.

"We've just seen something utterly unique," says Jake to Bigsy, who nods.

"Let's hope Melship and Lessiter are both here somewhere!" says Bigsy.

Jallie T and her band were already rocking their way through the next number.

Breakfast with dark glasses

The next morning, at breakfast, there was no sign of Hannah and Lottie, nor of Christina.

Lottie had texted Clare to say that she and Hannah had both been summoned to their respective MPs, for a briefing before they left for Gstaad.

It wasn't until lunch time that they returned and could explain what was happening.

"First of all, that was a fantastic experience yesterday!" said Hannah, "I mean, to be on stage with Jallie and Christina. To get some part of that applause."

Lottie added, "But I'm amazed how they could just carry on after that single number. It was immense and intense. Oh yes, and I noticed that Tony the Motor seemed impressed too, especially with you Hannah!"

"Did you tell Duncan you were on stage?"

"I wasn't sure about that," answered Lottie, "He might have wondered how I'd come to be in that position."

"To be honest, so was I!" said Hannah, "I've never done anything like that before, never, ever!"

"Stick with us, Hannah!" said Clare, "We may drive a twisty road but it's a lot of fun."

"And now we've got to prepare for the ski interlude! Jake, I know you ski, and Bigsy a bit, since that holiday last year. Christina is a natural, all that time in Iceland and Russia I suppose, and I assume the same for Antanov. But what about you, Lottie? And Hannah?"

Lottie answered, "Growing up, learning to ski was a bit like going to school. Mandatory. My father was able to get over the fact that I hadn't inherited his hand-eye coordination because I let him lead me down La Sarenne – The Alps' longest black run, at 18km (11 miles)—aged 10."

Lottie continued, "A year later, he took me to Gstaad, where he himself had learned to ski. Any photographs I took on our father-daughter trip are long gone, but memories stick in my mind. The chocolates we brought back, our patience waning as the shop assistant diligently wrapped the boxes up in similarly painstaking style to the jewellery salesman in Love Actually. The drive from Vevey, where some of my grandmother's family lived, each bend in the road that hugged the towering mountains revealing another majestic view."

She added, "Finally, Gstaad itself – demure chalets with generations-old, rich decoration along the widely projecting roofs and carved balconies; traditional horse-drawn carriages clip-clopping down the main cobbled street; glamorous women, all kept in check by the impossibly romantic Palace Hotel, from its voyeuristic perch high above."

"And you, Hannah?"

"When I was young, I had a ski-teacher who learned to ski around Chamonix. Like a lot of his colleagues and his father before him, he's a dairy farmer. In summer, he escorts his precious herd – 'his princesses' – into the high, verdant pastures. In winter, as pasture becomes piste, the cows retreat to the warm safety of a hay-stuffed barn, leaving him free to instruct and guide."

"They are both amazing stories," said Bigsy, "So now you'll have to tell us what the big boys wanted?"

Hannah answered, "Lessiter and Melship? They wanted to know the arrangements to get us up to Gstaad - what kind of car - that kind of thing."

Hannah looked in her notepad, "It turns out that the special guests are being ferried up to Gstaad in a variety of supercars and other specialist vehicles. "

"How the other half live," muttered Bigsy.

Hannah continued, "I hope I've got this right...Melship asked for a Bentley Bentayga - which I'd never heard of - but has got a Lamborghini Urus - a silly name designed to appeal to the Russians, I'm told. Lessiter asked for an Aston Martin DBS Superleggera but they had to point out to him that although it has four seats, it is somewhat cosy in the back. He insisted and so he now has two cars to take his party to Gstaad. The Aston and an all-electric Ford Mustang SUV."

"Let's hope that news doesn't get back to the UK then," said Jake, "Embarrassing pictures of MPs in sports cars in Switzerland!"

Hannah continued, "Many of the assistants are travelling on a few all-electric coaches, called eCitaros, which I suppose are more environmentally friendly."

Jake said, "I guess we will hear when the supercars start arriving this afternoon, but first we've got that session about reconfigurable electric drive matrices."

"Oh, I'm supposed to go to that, as well. It's obvious that Lessiter and Melship have brought Lottie and me to be their scribes."

"We'll, at least there is some free time as well," mused Jake, "Rock Goddess or Research Assistant"

"Good point!"

"Maybe more free time when we all get to Gstaad?" said Jake.

"I'm not holding my breath," said Hannah.

Reconfigurable Electric Drive Matrix (REDM)

Jake and Hannah finish breakfast and walk outside and along a snow-cleared route into the main presentation hall. The change to crisp alpine air wakes them both up.

Jake says, "This air when we walk back to the Palexpo; it's like a jolt of coffee."

"I agree," says Hannah, "I'm less sure how some of those lightly dressed female demonstrators are coping."

Jake looks at Hannah, "You know, Tony, he's a good mate of mine, but - how can I put this - he's kind of flexible when it comes to women."

Hannah smiles, "I know, I realised from right back in your office when he was making with the eyes. This is a car show and I'm only taking him for a test run."

Jake smiles back at Hannah, "Good, I'm relieved, I wouldn't want him to be hurting anyone."

"No, I can look after myself. Really."

Jake made to change the subject, "Here we are, Reconfigurable Electric Drive Matrix (REDM) - benefits and applications"

On stage was a car chassis. It had a recognisable front and back, but the part in the middle was a simple flat area.

"Bigsy was right," says Jake, "It does look like a toy Scalextric car without the body on it."

"So, in the future we'll all be buying the same chassis with different styling applied?" says Hannah, "They are determined to make cars boring."

On stage were four 'scientists' in white coats and two other bubbly presenters who looked like they could be on a children's TV show.

"Hi, I'm Greta and I'm Jonas," they said in unison.

Jonas bounced on the stage as if he was about to perform an amazing card trick with balloons and fireworks.

He starts: "The models of the future e-Auto family are currently being developed on the basis of the new reconfigurable electric drive matrix (REDM)."

Jake's and Hannah's shoulders sagged under the realisation that this would be like the batteries, brake fluids, or the tyre presentations that they had previously attended.

Greta picks up and continues with the exposition, "These are vehicles in a variety of classes which have been designed as full electric vehicles and reach ranges of up to 500 km and more. The architecture of the REDM will fundamentally change electric cars and cars in general."

Jake mutters, "Sales pitch,"

Jonas adds, "The REDM Toolkit jettisons all the ballast of the fossil age because it has been designed throughout for electric cars. This leads to fundamental changes in body design, interior design, the package and the powertrain characteristics of electric vehicles."

Now they walk around the car's frame pointing out different and somewhat obvious features.

- The wheels (but thinner tyres than usual for improved economy).
- The engines (electric and on each axle - two for the rear wheels and one for the front because of the complication of steering).
- The wiring (Two big fat cables from the front of the car to the back - for fault tolerance).
- The automatic self-diagnosing display (would alert to errors even before they

became serious).

- Autonomous driving (but with plenty of caveats)
- Safety detectors (even checks whether the driver is dozing off)
- The huge bank of batteries which would give the vehicle a claimed 300 miles.

"I could have written most of this without attending the session," says Jake.

Hannah nods her agreement. "It is pretty basic, and we only have their words for most of these things."

Jonas continues, "We want to establish REDM as an industry standard. We have opened the reconfigurable electric drive matrix to other manufacturers. This makes production cheaper, but also offers further advantages. You will find we are open to e-collaboration.

Greta adds, "The REDM is a decisive plus point"

Then Jonas, "The battery is considered the heart of modern electric cars. We can stretch this floor pan and it becomes a van with a 350-mile range, or a microbus able to seat eight people in comfort. Such a microbus could revolutionise inner city travel."

The first of the white coats was standing. Jake nudges Hannah and looks towards the exit. She nods and they both slink out of the auditorium, along with around fifty other people.

"Coffee?" says Hannah.

They make their way to a small coffee area set up for delegates who were between sessions. There was a 'push the lever' coffee machine which filled small paper cups with strong coffee.

They seated themselves at a quiet table.

"I could have made most of that up from the brochure," says Hannah, "I just hope Lessiter and Melship are becoming more knowledgeable."

"But we've hardly seen them?" observes Jake.

"Haven't you realised?" says Hannah, "They are having a blast, being wined and dined by manufacturers in separate hospitality suites. Several of the hotels around here have been taken over and suppliers and manufacturers have a floor each, in which to schmooze with their clients."

"I should have known," says Jake, "I could have looked out for the signs."

Hannah laughs,"...Martha Ford Suite? Carl Benz Suite? Frank Seiberling Suite? Zündapp Suite? Ford, Mercedes, Goodyear, Porsche. If you get my drift."

Jake laughs, "I may have been out of journalism for just too long," he said.

"Well, here's something else I picked up, " says

Hannah. She was just about to begin when Christina and Bigsy appear with Antanov Chekeryn.

"Look who I found in the main hall!" says Christina as Antanov introduces himself to Hannah.

"Er - are you Russian?" asks Hannah, "Only with that name...I could never tell it from your accent!"

"Yes, I'm originally from the far away land, from Perm, which is in the Volga. But when I was quite young, my parents moved to Moscow and then later to Saint Petersburg. I was at the same Akademy as Christina in Arkhangelsk - we run into one another every few years!"

Jake smiled as he thought how difficult it would be to believe that story, yet how true he knew it to be.

"I was just explaining to Christina how I'd found out a few things about one of the car companies that your MPs are going to visit."

Hannah looks surprised, "How could you know about that?" she asks.

"Christina and I trust each other with information. It can be very useful when trying to work out certain complicated situations."

Jake nods, "That's right, I remember when Antanov was in London that time, and provided us with all manner of useful facts and contacts for some work we were doing with another organisation."

"But if you are linked with the secret service?" asks Hannah, "Surely Antanov isn't as well?"

"No, I'm not," answered Antanov, "But I have my own set of contacts and am very comfortable to work with Christina. When we have flown helicopters together over the Dvina River and the White Sea, then you put trust in one another.

"Kotyonok, you remember when I rescued you from the fishing hut near Kumbysh? and I certainly remember you hauling me back from the Paratov Restaurant in Archangel, to help me avoid a court martial."

Christina laughs, "Yes this is the man who turned up in a helicopter to rescue me when my dingy washed up on an island just before the White Sea. Then at another time, I had to fetch him in a taxi, when he'd fallen in with a crowd of drunken sailors and 'gone fishing' in the city. He was so drunk he could not stand up. I hauled him back to our base, carried him up a fire escape and tucked him into bed."

They both laugh. Hannah looks confused, "Is there anyone who Clare knows that is kind of 'normal'?

Bigsy answers, "If you have to ask then it is probably you - although after your singing and pom-poms on Lac Leman, I think you are safe."

"Well, let me tell you what I found out!" says Antanov, "And I had to pull strings to get some of this. Antanov opened a small laptop and began to read.

"It's a long story all about Zillian's rise from the rubble", he says, "Brace yourselves:

"Weidemotoren was a manufacturer of tractors, agricultural machinery and engines, founded in 1933 by industrialist Tomas Weide in the Landsberg district of Bavaria.

"It was the beginning of considerable development of Weide's factories. Coincidentally, another tractor company was also started in Bavaria around this time. Both companies made tests and carried out competitive work.

"By 1936, the other company - Eicher - built the first diesel tractor with a 20 hp Deutz - diesel engine. The gearbox was attached to the engine and passed the power via a propeller shaft to the rear axle.

"Weide saw the design and a few inherent problems, and built a vastly improved version, with selectable engines and transmissions in 1937.

"In the same year, Weide was represented for the first time at the DLG (Deutsche Landwirtschafts-Gesellschaft) exhibition in Munich. The modular construction of tractors with flexible engine choices was an instant hit and prevailed in the following years. "

"They have a whole show for tractors?" asks Jake.

"Oh, it's immense, says Antanov, "There's even a spin-off of the show in Russia - It's called 'Potato Days, Russia!' "

Jake looks incredulous.

Antonov continues, "And if you go to one of their DLG Feldtage - sorry, field days - you'll be able to see actual kit operating on real fields. Think of a car show only with tractors!"

He smiles as he notices the look of fear that briefly flickers across the faces of Jake and Hannah.

Hannah interrupts, "Yes, that is consistent with what I found out from a briefing with Douglas Lessiter and Duncan Mclship yesterday. It ties in with some things about Zillian, but I'd better let you continue, Antanov," she smiles and then felt the full force of Antanov's charm beaming back.

Jake realises that Hannah and his buddy Tony Brooklands were evenly matched in the flirtation department.

Antanov continues, "Weide decided to diversify and became an automobile manufacturer in 1938 when it purchased Fahrzeugfabrik Nieten, which, at the time, built Morris 8s under licence under the Nieten marque as the well-known Nieten Luxus."

"I've seen pictures of them. I think it was an early example of the use of common running platforms, to build a saloon, a tourer and even a van or small truck," says Bigsy, "It's strange how history is re-inventing itself now."

Antanov looks back at his laptop, "The onset of war caused the retooling of the Weide factory for the additional production of armaments and aircraft engines to a generic design also produced in other factories throughout Germany.

"Weide's factories were heavily bombed during the war and its remaining West German facilities were banned from producing motor vehicles or aircraft after the war.

"The company survived by making agricultural tools and bicycles as well as pots and pans. In 1948, following BMW restarting motorcycle production Weide was able to restart its own vehicle production.

"Weide resumed car production in 1952 with the Nieten Weide luxury saloon and a lighter 2-door version. The range of cars was expanded in 1955, through the production of the cheaper Wespe 3-wheeler microcar under licence.

"Slow sales of luxury cars and small profit margins from microcars meant BMW was able to completely outpace Weide until BMW, too, became in serious financial trouble and in 1959 the BMW company was nearly taken over by rival Daimler-Benz.

"The faltering Weide was almost saved by an

industrialist, Günther Quandt, but with the influence of his sons, they placed their entire investment with BMW instead."

Antanov continues, "We should note some background. Günther Quandt joined the Nazi party in 1933 and made a fortune arming the German Wehrmacht, manufacturing weapons and batteries.

"Quandt's enterprises were appropriated from Jewish owners under duress with minimal compensation.

"At least three of Quandt's enterprises made extensive use of slave labourers, as many as 30,000 in all. One of his battery factories had its own on-site concentration camp, complete with gallows. Life expectancy for labourers was six months. It is alleged that it was the funds amassed in the Nazi era by his father which allowed Herbert Quandt to buy and rescue BMW."

"Yes," confirms Hannah, "it's like what I heard as well, although they didn't mention the Nazi influence and made the BMW bail-out sound like a rich family purchase."

Antanov continues, "This bleak situation left Weide to fend for itself and without investment, it moved back to its origins, producing tractors. In 1948, the first post-war development was finally presented, the Weide 16.

"This tractor used an air-cooled diesel engine. The

same multi-platform technique was used with Weide producing more tractors with increasing horsepower - the imaginatively named Weide 25, 28 and 30 - each able to carry a more sophisticated range of tools."

The Germans seemed to like air-cooled designs," observes Bigsy, "Think of the Volkswagen Beetle or the early Porsches".

"Porsche's last air-cooled car was the 993," sas Jake, "See? I do remember some things from my time at Street. I had to do a filler article on one once, I remember that Keanu Reeves, David Beckham, Harry Styles, Ellen Degeneres, and Antonio Banderas, all had them."

"We are drifting off topic," says Christina, " I know, Jake, you want to prove you haven't lost the street cred,"

Antonov laughs, "Well it's more interesting than me just running through this history lesson. The Weide marque continued through the 50s and 60s, creating tractors and tools such as flail mowers, backhoe loaders, stone buriers, rotovators, hedge trimmers, cultivators, ploughs, log splitters and power harrows."

'Stone buriers?" says Jake.

"We'll be testing you on what each one does, at dinner," jokes Bigsy.

Antonov adds, "But now the clever idea. Their designs retained the modular concept with the advantage that the tractor attachments would work with either the Ferguson 3-point hitch or the Euro adapter using something called the A-hitch."

"I see, so they could hook up to anything, " says Bigsy.

"Story of my life," says Jake.

"Boys, let's be serious," says Christina.

Antanov continues, "Weide A-hitch patents were licensed to many other tool suppliers and the run-rate of licensing deals kept the company alive for the next fifty years.

"In 2016, Weide was sold in a surprise takeover by Zillian Automobile. Analysts declared the takeover as mercenary and that Zillian wanted to buy 'heritage' for its new startup business."

"I see, says Jake, "It's like Lamborghini, able to show its early credentials in tractors and even batteries before moving to automobiles.

"Yes, except these new Zillian credentials would be faked," answers Antanov.

"And they have side-stepped the war implications, too" says Hannah, "And now, I've found out a few things too. It wasn't actually from Zillian, but from one of the well-known car companies trying to run interference on Zillian."

"How so?" asked Jake,

Hannah replied, "Oh, Lottie and I have had a string of invitations to all kinds of 'meet the people' sessions because we are representing Lessiter and Melship. One was with a mega corporation who want to bring ever larger trucks to the UK.

"It was an embarrassing session when someone pointed out that they would not fit under UK's motorway bridges. The bridges are 4.7 metres high, but these new curtain-sided trucks were 5 metres high!"

"However, those present started to chatter about competition and a string of scandals were implied.

Hannah continues, "There was a whole somewhat juicy section about Zillian and Weide. It turns out the combined car maker firm has been mired in controversy, corruption, sleaze, and sex scandals ever since the takeover by Zillian.

"Industry experts say the 'Unterlech Fortress Mentality' - the town where the company has its headquarters - made arrogant bosses feel invincible in the face of competition and regulation.

"To be honest, this didn't ring true with me. It looked more as if the Weide company had been honest manufacturers of tractors and then had a lucky break with that connector licensing deal.

"I felt that the sleaze was being pumped in from the Zillian direction. As an example, In 2019, it was the centre of a sex scandal which rocked Germany. Zillian's Workers' Council chief, Meik Meindl, received £1.2million in bribes, some of which paid to his Brazilian lover Miriam Conceição de Ávila

"To improve their chances, Zillian organised sex parties for German MPs and union bosses. Former personnel manager Franz Rimensberger admitted his role in the scandal. And this was in the time when Zillian was only making a handful of cars."

"I could see it would be a quick way to climb to the top," says Jake, "That's to the top of a rather sleazy pole, of course."

Hannah continues, "A €5 billion compensation fund was set aside as bosses braced for the raft of collective compensation claims from customers who purchased unfit vehicles - frequently because of emissions claims."

"So what vehicles was Zillian producing at that time?" asks Bigsy, "I thought Zillian was all about electric cars?"

"Yes, it is, " answers Hannah, "The cars in question are all from Weide, but now rebadged as Zillian. The 303, which looks quite like a Mini Cooper, the 404, which is quite like a medium sized BMW, and their bigger car, the 505, which looks like a Range Rover."

Antanov adds, "The cars were only making 'placeholder sales' in Europe and the USA at that time. Enough to keep the marque validated, but not enough to turn a profit. Our investigations suggest that the cars were actually rebadged Chinese copies of European cars."

"Ha," says Bigsy, "A rebadged Chinese car then rebadged as a Zillian."

"That's right," says Antanov, "Zillian are simply buying Chinese cars to resell as Zillian, while they became established in the market."

Jake asks, "What like the JAC A6, which is a rip-off of the Audi A6? - I only learned about it this week!"

"That's right," says Hannah, looking at her notes, "Even the Rolls-Royce Phantom is available as a copycat from China - the Geely GE - although they later had to restyle it and change the name to EmGrand."

Jake asks, "But surely this is another point of suspicion about Zillian, then?"

Hannah continues, "Yes, they wanted keep Zillian looking like a German company, but it didn't help when their chief executive Carl Tisch resigned, saying he wanted to give the German manufacturer 'a fresh start', after the allegations of copycat cloning and emission result faking."

Hannah adds, "But Zillian is no stranger to

controversy. The latest to engulf Zillian rakes up painful memories for industry experts as the company's history is blighted by cover-ups, dodgy deals, and collusion. For example, in 2017, through Weide, the company shocked the markets by announcing it was taking a €160 million provision to cover losses it incurred as the victim of a foreign exchange fraud - almost halving its profits.

Hannah adds, "Look, I pulled some papers. That scandal, which led to an international manhunt for the fraudsters, caused Zillian shares to plunge almost a third. After a seven-month search, FBI agents arrested a foreign exchange broker from Frankfurt wanted in connection with the fraud, having tracked him to an apartment in Hollywood."

Antanov nods, "Yes, it is very similar to what I found out. He opened a hard bag and pulled out a small MacBook, which he then opened and turned around for everyone to see.

"I had it translated from German," he says, "It was in all the main papers at the time." He reads from the article:

'Shamed German MP Daniel Honigsman-Bopp attended a sex party organised by Zillian. He was jailed for perjury when he lied and said he hadn't attended.'

"That is hardly enough to discredit the company," says Antonov as he looked towards his next note:

"This situation centres on the collusion between union bosses and corporate bigwigs to keep the workers at the production lines and the profits rolling in."

Hannah interrupts, "Zillian was suffering from high wages, low productivity and increasing competition and wanted to push through harsh staff restructuring plans."

Antanov resumes, "That's what I discovered too, Hannah. Zillian's bosses knew their plans would be rejected if put to the Worker's Council and so set aside a €500,000 slush fund to entertain German politicians and union bosses to force them to agree to the reforms."

"I see, " says Christina, "Buy Weide to recredentialise Zillian, use cheap clone cars to establish a market, weaken the Union position to lay off staff - presumably Weide staff - and use a troubled company profile to weaken the price to make it cheap for a further take-over. These are all Kremlin plays from the old days. The young guys are throwing the old men out - again!"

Antanov continues, "Christina is right...The plan was to weaken the unions' clout by using honeytraps - in other words luring officials into compromising situations."

"This is so like the Minerva and Medusa programmes which ran in the UK, " says Jake.

Antonov adds, "Well this time they used company funds to pay for sex parties for powerful union reps and politicians. It looks like the Russian organised crime method of influence was being used by Zillian to influence German politicians.

"Daniel Herr, Zillian's personnel head, paid millions of euros over several years to the company's works council chief, Meik Meindl.

"Meindl used the money to fund lavish parties and luxury hotel stays in Brazil and Lisbon for shop stewards and disguised the payments as business expenses.

"Some €280,000 of the money was paid to Meindl's Brazilian lover, Miriam Conceição de Ávila, along with jewellery and furs. But the plot unravelled when the parties came to attention of state prosecutors after the actions of a whistle-blower.

"In the subsequent court case, Daniel Herr was fined €500,000, but escaped jail by admitting to his part in the affair.

"The court heard how he paid illegal bonuses to Meindl because Zillian's management 'wanted union acceptance to change of work practice.'

Christina says, "This a much simpler corruption - pure blackmail and payoffs. It comes straight from the age of old KGB training manuals."

Antanov nods, "German MP Daniel Honigsman-

Bopp was implicated in the fallout. He sat on the powerful IG Metall Union at Zillian in Augsburg where the workers' committee and staff reforms required his approval.

"Honigsman-Bopp later admitted being present at a Sexworld party in a Hanover club, where champagne and 'other entertainment' were laid on for workers' council directors.

Hannah says, "As far as I can tell, in the same year, Zillian was also caught up in a corruption scandal in India when a senior executive promised to build a factory in the Andhra Pradesh state in return for a €1.4m payment."

Clare smiles. She knows Hannah is an awesome researcher and now Hannah was allowing herself to freewheel, she was finding out all kinds of interesting facts.

Hannah adds, "And further, the company was embroiled in a wider auto industry corruption scandal after executives at some carmakers were accused of taking bribes from suppliers.

"This scandal led to the resignation of the executive chairman of Vitless, a French brake component maker, after Erwin Lang, Zillian chief executive at the time, threatened to sever ties with the company."

Antonov adds, "After this, Red Fox - a subsidiary of Brant Holdings - were raided as part of an investigation into alleged market manipulation by the company's executives during a failed takeover of Zillian."

"Whoa, Whoa, Whoa," says Jake, "Brant. Again, involved in malpractice. I thought we had stopped all of that."

Christina smiles, "Think of that fairground game.... Whack-a- Mole. Brant is like that and will keep reinventing itself to pop up again."

Hannah adds, "Yes. The industry insiders at the briefing suggested that Brant quietly built a stake in Zillian by using a contentious options strategy, which distorted the price of Zillian's ordinary shares over a multi-year period. They used Red Fox to do this, so that they could appear 'hands off' if anything became difficult.

Then she referred to her notes, "Joachim Ganser, president of the association of German industries, BDI, said; 'We strongly criticise any form of manipulation. Any misconduct must be cleared up completely with transparency, openness, and speed.

Hannah looked at her notes again, " 'Made in Germany' stands for excellent products,' Ganser said, adding that German engineering and craftsmanship were 'rightly respected worldwide'. Deutsche Nachrichten, the broadcaster reported that 'Ganser's statement reflects deeper concerns here in Germany that Zillian's breach of industry ethics could do lasting damage to the country's reputation as a producer of top-notch goods.'

Jake summarises, "Okay, so our two MPs are both chatting away amiably to a remarkably dodgy car manufacturer."

Hannah adds, "I wish that was all. They have also both been happy to visit all kinds of hospitality events whilst here in Geneva and have sent myself and Lottie away to attend seminars about automatic transmissions and the advantages of winter tyres."

Antanov smiles, " I must congratulate you, Hannah, to not be fooled by this although I suspect much of your material also required additional research?"

"Yes, it did, after I knew a few key points and therefore where to start digging. I also borrowed the help of an industry expert who seemed happy to assist my line of enquiry."

Jake smiles, realising that Tony had not been leading Hannah along. It was more the other way around.

Bérénice Charbonnier

Late afternoon, the invited delegates for the Gstaad session had all been transported to Hotel Les Bergues, on the lakeside in Geneva. There was a gentle clinking of champagne glasses while they waited for their cars. They had all gone together and were now working the senior delegates before they made their way to Gstaad.

The outside of the hotel has been dressed to look like a pit-stop, complete with grid girls and even some grid guys. The first of the cars were already being filled with people, and by the sound of them they were powerful petrol driven cars. Polar opposites of the vehicles being promoted by the car manufacturers.

"It's hilarious to watch," says Lottie as a silver saloon with two rows of slit-like headlights came into view. It had a huge V-shaped cheese grater front grill and made a rasping sound with its 3.5 litre twin-turbo V6 engine.

"But listen as they describe the paint colours too," says Hannah, "Dragon Orange Metallic, Sao Paolo Yellow, Thermal Orange Pearl, Cyber Orange, Phoenix Yellow, Ocra Tri-Coat, Lime Essence, Papaya Spark. Imagine ticking the wrong box in the dealership?"

Lottie replies, "I guess they are all televisual colours - like the Mamids wear on those review shows."

Jake queries, "Mamids? - I've heard of Mamils - Middle Aged Men in Lycra - not so much the Mamids?"

Christina answers, "Middle aged men in denim."

Jake smiles, since he'd left Street, he was losing touch with his Urban.

Lottie had been asked to stay with Duncan Melship and Hannah with Douglas Lessiter for the car collection, although they both knew they had been relegated to separate cars for the journey to Gstaad.

Clare was with Christina when she noticed Tony Brooklands among those at the reception and wandered over to say 'Hello'.

"Oh hello, Clare," he replied, "Are you excited to be in one of the most high-value car processions that Geneva has seen?"

Clare smiled back, 'Boys and their toys,' she was thinking.

Tony was talking to another group of people and he briefly introduced them as Bérénice Charbonnier from le Genevois - the Geneva newspaper, Kjeld Nikolajsen, Miller McDonald and Mary Ranzino from Brant and Qiu Zhang and Volvakov Kirill Valeryevich representing Zillian.

"It sounds as if these two companies want to make a big splash with electric cars," says Tony, "It is most exciting."

"My card," says Volvakov Kirill Valeryevich, "And you may call me Kirilka,"

He hands them both an embossed card, with one side printed in Russian and the other in English.

They also notice that Bérénice Charbonnier was adroitly ushering the group, including Tony, away from them both.

Christina whispers, "There's such an obvious Russian-style game-play being used here, although I'd say that Qiu Zhang works for the Chinese MSS and it is a copycat model.

"The MSS?" queries Clare, "That's a new one on me,"

"The Ministry of State Security (MSS), or Guoanbu is the civilian intelligence, security and secret police agency of the People's Republic of China, responsible for counterintelligence, foreign intelligence and political security. MSS has been described as one of the most secretive intelligence organisations in the world. It is headquartered in Beijing."

Christina continues, "I had to check it out once before. The MSS facilities operate from close to the Summer Place in Beijing. The MSS is divided into secretive Bureaus, each assigned to a division with a broad directive. The Enterprises Division is responsible for the operation and management of MSS owned front companies, enterprises, and other institutions."

Clare asks, "You seem to know a lot about this."

Christina nods, "Yes, I'd almost forgotten, but the other time I checked MSS out, it was beginning to copy the way Russia became more gangster-like. Like when the Russian state apparatus created all their offshore companies, sent trusted people to run them, launder money through them and then appoint other people to take over the state banks and heavy industries like oil, minerals, and logistics. The old guard ran everything until the young guns wanted more of the pie and started throwing the old men off balconies. Nowadays, like in so many things, the Chinese are trying to copy the processes."

Christina adds, "I've had a prior run-in with Bérénice too. Don't be taken in by her warm smiles. She has ice running through her veins. I suspect she is in the pay of the Chinese, orchestrated by Qiu Zhang."

"Wow, we got a lot from that 30 second meeting with Tony!" says Clare.

They were nearly at the front of the line to pick up their cars to be transported to Gstaad.

Cars to Gstaad

Duncan Melship's car arrived first. It had a Lamborghini badge on the front but looked like a yellow SUV.

"I doubt if that is what Melship was expecting!" mutters Tony, under his breath.

"It reminds me of one of those Porsche people carriers you see all around London," agrees Bigsy.

"Astute," breathes Tony, "It uses some of the same bits inside."

Melship climbs into the car, along with two smiling women in matching yellow jumpsuits.

"It's the London scene being played out here in Geneva," says Bigsy, "Eye candy for the men in suits,"

"And the research assistants have to follow up on the bus," adds Clare.

The car accelerates away from the hotel, just as a somewhat sleeker car arrives, announced as a lime essence green Aston Martin, followed by a red Ford SUV.

"It must be Duggie's car," says Hannah and watches as he steps forward, along with another two remarkably slim women.

"It's so they can fit in the back," explains Jake, "The opposite of 'supersize'.

Sure enough, Duggie was led by the hand to the low-slung Aston Martin and then had to assist as the two women slid into the small back seats.

"What a business!" muses Bigsy, then looking startled as he realised, he'd said it out loud.

Suddenly, an unmistakable bright red Ferrari appeared to a few gasps from the crowd.

"My ride," says Christina.

"I approve," utters Tony as Christina strode toward the vehicle, "You are looking at a £500k plus car over there," he said, "I think it does 0-60 in under three seconds."

"But can it handle snow?" asked Jake, "Or is it only good along la Croisette and outside Senequier?"

"No ladies for Christina," observes Clare.

"But there's nowhere to fit them," says Bigsy, laughing.

"Shall we make our way to the buses?" asks Clare.

"Good plan," says Lottie.

Snow crunches under their feet as they approached the bus shelters, where a fleet of electric buses was marshalled to take the less privileged assistants to Gstaad.

PART TWO

Ed Adams

Toblerone

Ice cream.

That is all.

Bigsy

About Gstaad

"It really is the land of chocolate and cheese, here in this part of Switzerland," observes Bigsy.

"And small ski resorts," adds Jake.

They had disembarked from their coach at Le Grand Bellevue hotel.

Gstaad–once described by Julie Andrews as 'the last paradise in a crazy world'– to find out what lies behind the jet-set façade.

"This isn't for normal people," observes Jake.

   "It's amazing," adds Clare.
   "Are we really staying here?" asks Bigsy.

A woman appeared, "Welcome to Gstaad. Let's get you sorted out," She handed each of them a small guidebook and yet another lanyard and badge.

Jake scanned the copy on the guidebook cover:

"It's the skiing that many return to Gstaad for, year after year – 200km (124 miles) of immaculately groomed, wide and often empty slopes. Unlike other popular resorts, Gstaad's ski areas are separated by nature reserves and un-pisted mountain faces. Far from being inconvenient, it means spending each day in a new area, exploring new terrain, from the windswept plateau of Glacier 300 – the only glacier ski area in the Bernese Oberland – to the Wasserngrat's Tiger Run, the region's steepest slope with an average gradient of - 45°."

A voice interrupts his reading, "If you could each identify your luggage, we will arrange to have it shipped to your suites and chateaux. Some of you will need to catch further small bus to your individual chateau."

"I guess that will be us, then," says Clare, "I imagine this hotel is for the more well-heeled and influential."

As if on cue, both Lessiter and Melship appear, surrounded by a small posse of cat-suited women. Lessiter seemed to be enjoying the attention, although Clare sensed a look of work-weariness in the eyes of the women.

Lessiter was being shown to a room, and Melship was waiting patiently for his key. Clare noticed that these guests seemed to get a whole carrier bag full of goodies, instead of the guidebook that they had received from the coach disembarkation.

"I feel this is the kind of place that James Bond would like," observes Bigsy.

"Silly, this is exactly the place where Roger Moore, 007, lived in real life," says Lottie, " I think he moved from this side of the mountains to the other side, to Crans-Montana, which has even more skiing," answers Hannah.

"Impressive," says Bigsy, absent-mindedly, "Oh I'm sorry, I keep saying things I'm thinking, out loud!"

They all laughed. Hannah adds, "I've just been reading the guidebook. It happens to mention Roger Moore in it. But he's not the only celebrity - in fact, there's whole herds of them!"

Jake laughs, "Herds, an interesting collective noun for celebrities! I'm thinking a clique, or maybe a pap?"

An official-looking woman appeared. "You are together?" she asks, "I have a 16-berth chalet which you can occupy."

They all looked at one another, nodded and Jake says, "Yes, do lead the way,"

The woman took them to a Mercedes Coach, and then they made their way a short distance to a huge chalet overlooking the valley.

"I could get used to this life-style," says Bigsy.

They were greeted at the door by Allegra Schrämli, who announced herself as the chalet maid.

"Unbelievable," says Bigsy, out loud. The others smile.

"Willkommen, Bienvenue," said Allegra, "I've fixed for you all to have a fondue this evening made with the finest Gruyere from the Pays-d'Enhaut. After a day like today, it will be something cosy and social for you all before business starts again tomorrow!"

She waved them into the wooden chalet which was stunningly appointed in a modern architectural style, "Oh, wow, I wasn't expecting this," says Jake, "Oops, I've caught Bigsy's speaking out loud thing!"

"It is architect-designed, like many of the larger chalets. I sometimes think the bigger guests miss out when they all want to stay in the major hotels here. This chalet was designed by Chaletwirth Architekten and the inside was furnished by Alexandra Bernardette, that most famous designer."

"But komm," she says, "Choose your rooms; there are few enough of you to ensure that everyone will get a balcony with a view. And there is a ski-room downstairs where you can grab some kit for the slopes."

"Pinch me," says Bigsy to Clare, "Am I dreaming all of this?"

Clare's phone rang. It was Christina.

"Hiya Ms Ferrari, are you nicely settled in your luxury hotel? We've done well with this overspill chalet which is as top of the range as you can imagine. It even includes skis."

"That's what I wanted to call you about," says Christina, "I've met with Antanov again. He's suggested we could all go skiing tomorrow."

"I'll need to check with the others, said Clare, "In case anyone wants to pass on it."

"Okay, well forget all those ski-lifts though. Antanov arrived at the hotel by helicopter. He says we can use it tomorrow to go heli-skiing. Apparently, there are six sites to choose from! What are they, Antanov?"

Clare could hear Antanov call out 'Gstellihorn, Wildhorn, Vordere Walig, Stalden, Gumm, Glacier de Tsanfleuron, but it's not a test!'

Clare realised that Christina and Antanov must be sharing a room, like that time in Germany.

Christina added, "I should also mention that Antanov has brought along a Mil Mi-171A2. It can take quite a few passengers and costs about 20 of my Ferraris!"

"I guess someone is taking this whole car thing quite seriously if Antanov can get hold of such kit?" asks Clare.

"Oh yes, not least because the Kremlin could be dragged through the mud for something it hasn't done. And let's face it with Antanov and me on the case, it has a certain high profile within Russia," answers Christina.

"And you know something? We should take Melship and Lessiter with us, see what we can find out," says Christina.

The right to disconnect

The next morning was Saturday, deemed a non-working day. The car Expo would start again on Monday, giving the delegates the weekend to unwind. This part of Switzerland was close enough to France to mean that some of the French customs of 35-hour working week and the 'right to disconnect' had been informally implemented.

Hannah and Lottie arranged for Melship and Lessiter to join the skiing expedition. Antanov had chosen to fly to the nearby Gsteig bei Gstaad area, which offered some low-risk skiing descents all through the valley toward Gstaad. Antanov estimated it was around 15 kilometres of gentle downhill to ski back and would not require any additional queues at cable stations.

Just as importantly, it ended in Gstaad, so the helicopter could be flown out but would not be needed for a subsequent pickup.

Clare invited Allegra to come along too, and they all

met at the Gstaad heliport, where Antanov's helicopter dwarfed the others present.

"It's difficult to hide something this large," exclaimed Antanov, "but it will give everyone the luxury experience."

Clare noticed that the helicopter's interior was a set of two clusters of four plump leather armchairs and then another two further back. It screamed luxury and she wondered if it belonged to an oligarch. She could not imagine the Kremlin's procurement department buying something so lavish.

Melship and Lessiter took it in their stride, and Clare quickly realised that they were being given the finest treatment by the various companies they were visiting.

They all settled into their newly acquired VIP suite, with Duncan Melship and Douglas Lessiter on the private chairs and then the rest of them filling in the cluster of eight seats, and with Christina Nott taking the co-pilot seat next to Antanov.

Clare noticed that Melship and Lessiter were talking between themselves and that they made little effort to socialise with the rest of the cabin.

Allegra looked in some wonder at the helicopter and appeared to be considering just who these guests were that she was supporting.

The skis and other paraphernalia had all been

loaded and then the 'copter took off and after what seemed like a few minutes was already preparing for a descent at the ski point.

Christina looked at ease in the co-pilot's seat and Clare remembered how Christina had told her about her military training in Arkhangelsk.

After a gentle landing, Antanov walked through the cabin.

"There," he said, "Just 15 kilometres from Gstaad, but a totally different outlook. After you have unloaded, Christina and I will take the plane back to Gstaad and see you in a couple of hours for après ski."

Helipad

They disembarked and Clare noticed the other people around the helipad. In a fashionable ski outfit, Bérénice Charbonnier was standing with Qiu Zhang and Volvakov Valeryevich. Behind them, a small group of additional men, who Clare considered to be their minders.

Bérénice spoke,"*Quelle surprise, Une coïncidence, Et quel plaisir de vous voir. Nous avons pris le premier hélicoptère jusqu'à ce sommet, depuis Gstaad.*"

And then realising they were all English, "How great to see you all, we took the early helicopter to the peak, for a gentle ski back to Gstaad! Perhaps we can all go together?"

As if on cue, two more athletic looking women skied into view and joined Bérénice's party.

Clare could immediately spot the difference in ski capability among the group. Allegra, Christina and Antanov all looked fully proficient. Jake looked as if he could handle the skis well and at about the same level as Clare herself. She knew that Lottie took regular skiing holidays, so they should be good on the slopes. She could see that Bigsy was struggling to stay upright, as indeed was Lessiter. She'd judge Melship as a better skier and maybe around her own level.

By comparison Bérénice, Qiu Zhang and Volvakov Valeryevich all looked to be superior skiers, as did their entourage.

"We seem to have some mixed abilities here," said Jake, "I think you may enjoy a faster run toward the village."

"No, no, we wouldn't dream of it. We can probably help your group, too," replied Bérénice.

"Although whoever is last back gets the first round of schnapps!" said Volvakov.

Allegra called out, "I must remind my guests to stay safe. No excess speeds, stay away from the edges and beware equipment, low beams around the cable pylons and other sharp things on the descent."

Clare was impressed that Allegra had spoken up and wondered how mean seasons she had done as an instructor; she certainly moved gracefully on her skis.

Bérénice arranged them all into two rough groups.

"Here, we will make up the forward group and probably go slightly faster than the others. Then can come the middle group but I expect it will detach a few stragglers! No need to decide beyond the basic group yet!"

And with that, Bérénice, Qiu Zhang, Christina, Lottie and one of the minders took off down the slope

Then, the second group formed. Jake, Bigsy, Clare, Allegra, Lessiter and Melship, the two women, a minder and Volvakov.

"Okay, we can start now," said Volvakov, "Here, Douglas, why don't you ask my two pretty зайчонок to ski either side? They can catch you if you start to fall!"

He gestured to the two women, who he had just called 'little rabbits' in Russian. They both snuck up beside Lessiter as the second minder took an Instagram of them all together.

They set off down the mountain, more falteringly than the first group. After two kilometres it was apparent that this group contained several novices including both Melship and Lessiter.

"Don't worry," said Allegra, "There is a cable station about another three kilometres down this slope. Anyone that needs it can hire a sled from that point and ride down the remaining kilometres in style!"

Clare looked toward Melship, who already looked exhausted. By comparison, Bigsy was still looking fresh.

"You know, I'm quietly enjoying this and the pace is not too fast," he confided to Clare.

Soon, they reached the cable station, which had an adjacent Hire Store. From here they picked up several sleds and Melship, Lessiter, Bigsy and one of the women and the minder each put themselves into a sled.

"Lets's go now!" said Volvakov, and they gingerly released the brakes on the sleds and shot forward.

"This is the life!" said Lessiter, while the woman in another sled whooped encouragement.

Clare realised it would now be difficult to keep up and signalled to Jake to slow down.

"This is becoming something of a children's outing," whispered Jake and Clare smiled.

"It sure takes our minds away from the Car Show," said Clare.

In under an hour, they had reached the others, who were seated on a sun terrasse, sipping schnapps.

"Where did you get the karts?" asked Lottie, "Surely not at that cable station? You've hardly skied down at all if that is the case."

"We were just keeping with the transport theme," said Volvakov, waving his arm to attract a waitress, "Schlehengeist all around, please!"

"What's that?" asked Clare.

"Sloe berry spirit - a schnapps," answered Christina, "Perfect after skiing."

Clare sat down at the wooden bench with Melship and Lessiter.

"That was so exhilarating!" said Clare.

"Yes, it's another complicated one for the expenses," said Duncan. Douglas nodded his agreement. Clare looked at the two slightly drunken MPs. The altitude, exercise and schnapps had loosened both their tongues.

She asked, "Don't you ever worry? You know, like when the PM's house was decorated by a party donor? Or that MP who was working in the Caribbean? Full disclosure and all that?"

Lessiter laughed, "Oh yes. Full disclosure, always. But remember there is a difference between transparency and openness.

"It is possible to have the facts visible, but in ways that obfuscate the truth. Commons rules ensure MPs' earnings are publicly declared, but those rules also dictate that in the case of legal work only the firms need be named — not the clients, the people paying the bill. So, this time, to declare anything at all, I only need to show that the trip down the mountain was to support Brant Holdings."

Melship added, "He's right. MPs must declare 'any financial interest or other material benefit which a Member receives which might reasonably be thought by others to influence his or her actions, speeches or votes in Parliament.' And, by and large, they do. Sometimes the context isn't shown, like these lovely sun-drenched ski slopes."

Lessiter continued, "The register was the basis of much of the reporting on MP's second jobs. But the format in which it is published generates a fog that makes it enormously difficult to pick out the answers to many basic questions."

Melship expanded the theme, "For example, no one has been able to work out how much money MPs make from outside earnings since the last general election. And no one has worked out how much MPs made from, say, banking. Or law. The register is constructed as a riddle. Each MP's entry is published as a series of documents. They cover overlapping time periods, so the same interests will be declared time and again, making it rather confusing to unpick."

"But why are you telling me this?" asked Clare, looking confused. "I mean, you know I work in Parliament for Andrew Brading?"

Melship answered, "Yes, we both know. Andrew is one of the MPs who plays a completely straight bat. No scandal, no sleaze, a real goody two-shoes."

"Oh, no disrespect intended," hastily added Lessiter, "And I guess we could say that Parliament invented enigmatic accounting principles!"

Melship continued, "And we're telling you because none of this matters. We get a few presents from our sponsors. They expect to influence us. But the truth is each of us is only one six hundred and fiftieth of Parliament. By ourselves we can't do so much. But lobbying continues, we are just having some fun with it."

Lessiter added, "And the regulators inside Parliament know this too. Except for a few silly duck-houses and moat repairs, most of the system passes unnoticed. Most MPs' statements are a challenge to decipher. The data is unwieldy, unintuitive, and full of traps. To get the figures required for accurate analysis, you would need to manually go through every entry. The latest edition of the register shows MPs made close to 4,000 separate declarations of gifts, hospitality, and other outside interests. Since the last election it has been published and corrected many dozens of times."

Clare asked, "But doesn't this result in pseudo-transparency? Every MP has declared their second jobs. The information is published and accessible. But using that information is too time-consuming. The result? Less accountability and less scrutiny than if it were collected and presented in a modern, structured format."

Melship nodded, "I suppose we could publish it all in a spreadsheet for some of the newspapers, but then we'd lose out on all this sunshine and the rather marvellous schnapps...Cheers!!"

Jake and Lottie had been listening in on the conversation. It didn't leave either of the MPs looking good sat here among the car lobbyists.

Clare looked around. At other tables she could see equivalences of this group. Happy, drunken targets being hit upon with all manner of indiscretion. International lobbying at its finest. One could almost see it as a service industry.

Zopf

Morning. Sunday. The occupants of the chalet were emerging groggily to the breakfast prepared by Allegra.

"Here we are," Allegra announces, "Switzerland is the homeland of muesli, as we know it today. It was invented more than a hundred years ago by the local dietician Maximilian Bircher-Benner. It's so much more than a recovery food, one of the most popular breakfasts in the world!

"I prefer to put dried fruits in regular oat flakes, soaked in some water, milk or fruit juice and left overnight. You can also garnish with whole or chopped raw nuts of your choice.

"And it is Sunday. So, there is a tradition of Swiss braided bread called Zopf, garnished with marmalade and cheeses.

"Add Swiss croissants called gipfeli which are certainly the best company to your morning coffee.

And the king of croissants is His Majesty nusgipfel – A sweet muffin filled with walnut cream, which is generously covered with glaze on top.

"Not forgetting the rösti. A pancake of grated potatoes. it originated from the canton of Bern. The best thing about rösti is that it can be combined with any other type of breakfast such as eggs, bacon and so on. And the secret ingredient? Why nutmeg, of course.

"Enjoy!"

"I won't be able to move after all of that!" murmurs Jake to Bigsy.

"Oh, I will!" says Bigsy, grabbing a plate and moving in on the rösti, to which he added a couple of bacon rashers and a fried egg.

"Officially, today is a 'demonstration day' for the cars," explains Allegra, "You are supposed to go to the main area and select from the available vehicles to then be driven around the area. Why they chose the pedestrianised Gstaad for this I don't really understand!"

Clare smiles, "Maximising client contact time! Although I guess a lot of the people here are influencers rather than actual car buyers!"

"You'd be surprised," says Allegra, "Some of the people who live here or overwinter here are most definitely part of the global jet set. Add in a few of the visitors and there's a crazy full market for these luxury cars!"

"So, what will we do then?" asks Bigsy, "I guess we don't look like their typical car buyers."

"Why not go to the glacier?" asks Allegra, "You could take your MPs with you and they'll have a great time. My friend Jacques is in the company that runs the tours. I'm sure I can get you a Snow Cat and then you can take your group across the snow to the glacier."

"I guess it could 'break the ice' with them, they seem pretty much self-contained when they are around us," observes Clare.

"But how can we persuade them?" asks Jake, "I mean, they seem very plugged in to the official programme."

"Leave that to me," says Allegra.

Studded tyres

Two hours later, there was a commotion outside the chalet. Several cars had arrived. Clare noticed they had studded tyres, signifying they had been kitted out to traverse snow.

"My god!" utters Jake, "Have we stolen the whole car show?"

"No, we've just borrowed and diverted a few cars to come via our chalet. Jacques knows the car marshals and they simply took the next five vehicles and diverted them for us. But we must hurry, they will want them back!"

Jake surveys the cars. A McClaren 570S, a Porsche 911 4S, some kind of Ferrari. It says GTC4 Lusso on the back. That yellow Lamborghini SUV again and a Tesla S, which was apparently plaid, as if that was a good thing.

"It's 1100HP," calls Douglas Lessiter across to them.

Yes, Allegra had pulled off a great heist. Five luxury automobiles and two MPs, along with Christina and Antanov.

"How did you do it?" asks Clare, quietly to Allegra.

"I'm pretty well-known around Gstaad," answers Allegra,"I come from one of The Families, although I keep it quiet with visitors. As is my brother Jacques. All we need to do was ask the hotel concierge to route the two MPs to a special parking lot, where they could choose from five cars to get to the glacier. After that, it was easy. The drivers are all local, the cars are all insured to the best standards and have been booked out for one hour round trips. Speaking of which, we'd better get a move on. It'll take us twenty minutes to get to the foot of the glacier."

Soon enough, everyone was in a car, and as Allegra had predicted, the two MPs were happy to talk to their co-passengers. After all, this was a trip to remember.

And it had the added advantage that Bérénice Charbonnier and her friends were nowhere to be seen.

It's the glacier talking!

Hannah was in the car with Duggie Lessiter and Christina. Lessiter had specifically asked for Christina to join him.

Duncan Melship was with Lottie and Clare. Both MP's seemed entirely at home in their luxury cars, which Clare put down to a combination of over-indulgence in the privileged lifestyle and breakfast champagne.

"This is great!" said Duncan, "I didn't even see this listed in the programme; well done Lottie, for noticing it."

"I wouldn't mention this to too many of the other delegates," said Lottie, "I think we have received some privileged treatment courtesy of our friend Allegra."

"Right, this is happening to me all the time on this trip," replied Melship, "I'm not sure if I'll be able to report any of it when we get back!"

"You'll have my reports on tyre safety, reducing brake pollution and advanced battery technology, anyway," said Lottie.

"Ah yes, you've been doing a great job and the organisers were kind enough to supply a Word document which summarises every session. By the time we've worked that up into a report it should look comprehensive!" Melship smiled.

In the Tesla, which was following behind the Lamborghini used by Melship, Lessiter was talking to Hannah. They were both in the back seats, with Christina in the front passenger seat. Lessiter had insisted and even looked a little frightened by Christina.

"Hannah, thank you for getting those reports for me, you can see how busy I've been over the last few days. Tomorrow is the big meeting with Zillian, and I'd very much like you to attend. It's under the Non-Disclosure Agreement, because I think they want to let us in to some trade secrets."

Hannah nodded her assent, "Where is the meeting?" she asked, "Only it's not one of the ones scheduled?"

"I know; I had to keep it hidden. It was their insistence, a bit like this visit to the glacier doesn't seem to be on any of the schedules."

At that moment the Tesla made a sharp hairpin turn and Lessiter found himself squeezed against

Hannah's frame.

"Oh, I'm so sorry," he said looking awkward. "They say these cars drive themselves, they seem to have a few surprises too," He looked across to the driver, who merely grinned.

'Well, that dashes his hands reputation,' thought Christina. She had heard Clare relay the information from Rachel, which implied Lessiter had an altogether different orientation.

Soon they were at the foot of the glacier and the cars rolled up to the side of a large blue truck with enormous caterpillar tracks.

"That will be your next ride," explained the driver, "It has capacity for twenty people, so you should all be able to get window seats."

They climbed out of the car and watched the others with varying degree of struggle leaving their low-slung vehicles. Clare was quietly astonished that the lowest slung of them all, the McClaren, had even been able to drive through the snow without going aground.

They thanked the drivers and watched as the cars roared off, with the drivers deliberately disengaging the anti-skid devices so that they each threw up white arcs of snow.

"Wow! That was spectacular," uttered Lottie and Hannah nodded her head in agreement. They had all been given bulky red coats to wear for the next stage and as they climbed in, the driver explained, 'It's to be able to easily locate you if you get lost on the ice.'

He gave some other brief care announcements and they were off, bumping across the ice on caterpillar tracks. In the distance they could see another vehicle and the driver explained they would go to where the ice was still safe and where there should not be too many deep fissures.

"We will spend a few minutes walking around the glacier and then return to the Scex Rouge, which has restaurants and a sun terrace. If you want to, you can make an unforgettable walk across a suspension bridge between a couple of the 3000 metre peaks. On a clear day like today, you can see most of the Alps - Diablerets, Mont Blanc, Matterhorn and Jungfrau."

"And how do we get back from here?" asked Jake, "Once we are finished now that the cars have gone?"

"Oh, that's easy," answered Allegra, "I have arranged for a coach to pick us up from Col du Pillon, which is a cable car point. We take a cable car, then change to another one which will take us to the position. It is then a straight run back to Gstaad."

The Cat driver placed a short ladder against the side of the machine. Everyone climbed it and were soon travelling toward the glacier.

"A snow safari!" said Melship.

"Hopefully no wild animals!" answered Hannah.

Everyone laughed. Allegra had been right and the team bonding had begun.

They climbed out onto the ice and could see rivulets of blue water in the warm sunshine.

"Most of the fresh water on the planet is stored in glaciers, " said Allegra.

"But they are melting!" said Clare.

"Yes, the climate emergency is right here to see. This glacier has lost many metres of length in this century," answered Allegra, "Since 1850, the volume of Alpine glaciers has declined by about 60%.

"And in a single recent year, two heatwaves hit Switzerland between the end of June and late July, with around 30 degrees Celcius recorded in Zermatt. In 14 days of high temperatures, Alpine glaciers lost about 800 million tonnes of snow and ice, or the quantity of drinking water consumed by the entire Swiss population (8.5 million people) in the space of a year. But I didn't bring you all here to lecture about global warming! We should look at the view and experience nature."

They were all looking around, standing on the icy surfaces of the glacier, but noticing how much water lay everywhere.

"I suppose in a way all this has something to do with cars," said Melship wistfully.

Monday at the Gstaad expo

A crisp alpine morning and a new venue for the Expo at the hotel. Clare walked to the entrance where she met Christina and they both noticed the row of sparkling colourful sports cars parked outside.

"Someone has a de-icer for these," commented Christina., "Look at the normal cars!" She gestured to a couple of rows further back in the car park, where cars were parked in various states of snow-torment. Some were clear of snow, but others looked as if they had been hurriedly moved and, in some cases, still had snow on their roofs.

"Today it's the big meeting with Zillian," said Clare, "Remember we are only there as assistants."

"Tricky for me," answered Christina, "Remember I already know Bérénice Charbonnier, Miller McDonald Mary Ranzino and Qiu Zhang. I think I'd better make myself scarce."

Clare nodded, just as Lottie and Hannah appeared. They were both sporting new House of Common badges, which Christina noted.

"Cool badges?" she asked.

"The work of Bigsy. He reckoned only a few of us would get into the meeting, so he gave us these little things."

"Listening devices?" asked Christina.

"Yes, but transmitting to our phones, as well," said Lottie.

"You'll be careful in there?" asked Christina, "No heroics."

"Definitely not!" answered Lottie, she unclipped her badge, and showed Clare. It looked solid from the back and didn't show any trace of electronics.

"Bigsy said he got them from 'Amanda'," explained Hannah.

"There seems to be a lot of attention on this session," remarked Christina.

"Time to part company," said Christina as she walked toward the lobby area. She noticed Melship and Lessiter walking in, with someone else whom she didn't recognise. A man in a leather coat, with a small golden lapel badge. She listened to his speech and realised, by his accent, he was Russian.

Melship and Lessiter greeted Lottie and Hannah and the small group walked into the meeting room, except for leather coat man who stayed by the entrance.

"He's got an earpiece too," whispered Clare, who had also noticed the arrival. Christina smiled, "Let's test him."

She walked back through the crowded lobby to the entrance to the meeting room and asked the man, in deliberately broken English, "Excuse me, is this Tesla Meeting Room. I lost."

The man replied, "no, it is not here. You should ask at the information desk," he pointed.

"большое спасибо, bal'shoye spaseebah", answered Christina, and the man instinctively smiled.

"I see what you just did," smiled Clare, "He would have looked confused instead of giving you a polite smile, if he'd not understood."

"Okay, so we know the Russians are guarding the entrance to the meeting."

"There's something off about it though, " said Christina, "It's not how Russia does this kind of thing. We'd always have two people present. A guy on the door and another one to add some muscle if it were needed."

"I think I have your answer," said Clare, nodding to another man around six metres away from the Russian.

"Oh yes, you are right, I can see his earpiece too," said Christina,"You are getting good at this, Clare!"

"I've had lots of practice following you around, Christina!"

"But look," whispered Clare, "Does he look more Chinese to you?" she gestured toward the second man.

"Not necessarily," said Christina. She guided them both back toward the entrance to the building, adding, "Russia is a big place. He could come from the east. Maybe from Siberia. There are people with asian appearance from areas nearer China and the China-Russia border, at either end of Mongolia or the Gobi Desert. And don't forget there's another China-Russia border with North Korea."

They could see Jake and Bigsy now, close to the revolving doors to the building. It looked as if Bigsy was engrossed in a call.

"Hi," said Jake, "Bigsy is listening in, but he suggests that we should go to Christina's suite here in the hotel where we can all hear what is happening."

"It's okay, Christina gave me a key yesterday," explained Bigsy, "it's a pretty good suite too!"

He led the way to the elevators and eventually into Christina's Tower suite.

"It's huge," observed Jake, looking at the separate areas of the bedroom and the lounge area, flooded with light and a beautiful view toward the mountains.

"Yes, I set the speakers up in the lounge area, we can spread out on the sofas and listen to what is happening in the meeting. And don't worry, I'm recording it all," explained Bigsy.

"I'll order some coffee too," said Christina, as Bigsy switched on the system.

The speakers gave a low hum and then a voice came through,

'Before deductions, Zillian will raise approximately $6 billion, making it one of the biggest launches for a US company.'

The voice sounded American, "It's Miller McDonald," said Bigsy, "The Texan drawl gives it away."

'Isn't that a bit high for a car company that's only produced a dozen electric units this year?' asked a woman's voice.

"It's Mary Ranzino," said Clare.

Miller continued, 'You're not alone in thinking that. Indeed, our team says the figure looks incredibly high for any newly listed company, let alone one that only generated $1m of revenue in its most recent quarter.'

Now a Russian voice, 'The immense investor appeal may come from faith in the company's backers - notably that Brant has taken a deep position with Zillian, and soon we will have UK Government approval - so much faster than the EU, but just as marketable. Is that not right, Mr Melship?'

Melship replied, 'Well if these last few days are anything to go by, then I agree. And the share options that you are gifting to me and to Mr Lessiter make such a manoeuvre doubly attractive. If Zillian becomes engineered as a high growth prospect based upon electric vehicles, then we will need to compare it with other electric-vehicle companies and how they have fared after their IPOs.'

Mary Ranzino continued, 'A surge in share price is not unheard of for electric-vehicle IPOs. Tesla, along with Chinese carmakers Li Auto and XPeng, saw their share price increase more than 40 per cent on their first day of trading. Lucid Motors and Nio had more modest gains, but their share prices still closed 10 and 12 per cent higher than their IPO prices respectively.'

The Russian again, "How does this play out long term? If you prove you can deliver, you will be rewarded. But to achieve this you will need to make endorsements. And these endorsements need to come from people untainted with involvement."

"I can see why you have kept this meeting small and select," said Melship.

"And our assistants are very discreet,"

"It was very unfortunate, what happened to Isabella Stevens," said The Russian.

"That is such a clumsy threat," said Christina, "These people are watching too many American movies about making offers they can't refuse."

A new voice on the speakers asked, 'But how will we make this all seem credible? Zillian doesn't have any vehicles."

"I'm guessing that is Volvakov Kirill Valeryevich," said Christina, "he has a hint of a Russian accent."

'Kirilka,' said Mary, 'We may not yet, but the arrangement we have come to with Qiu Zhang means that Zillian can continue to supply plausible petrol cars until the electrics are ready. We will have a few nice but highly popular models which are almost undetectable from their European and American counterparts.'

'That's right,' said Qui Zhang,'We can manufacture any automobile clones required and in any volume. You'll need to provide us with plans, but we can turn the production facilities of several company towns over. They can produce the vehicles and if you want them badged Zillian, it can easily be achieved.'

Miller McDonald asked, 'But the industry and reporters are calling out for Zillian to show vehicles now. Even prototypes. And we need to do that to be able to run a floatation of the company.'

'That should not be a problem, we have two ideas for this,' answered Valeryevich, 'First we can use the Raft CGI platform to demonstrate the car.'

'In other words, you use a virtual car?' asked Melship.

'Secondly, we will acquire, legitimately, several eCar platforms and add new body skins. We'll soon have created the illusion that we are good to go,' said Mary Ranzino.

'Correct. Then a proposal...'

"Faking it?" said Jake, "Faking it to boost the share price."

Miller McDonald's voice continued, 'We will need a seal of approval. That is where you two come in, Mr Lessiter and Mr Melship. You will provide the legitimacy that the venerable Zillian needs to proceed.'

There was a pause. In Christina's room they all looked at Bigsy.

"Nope," he said, "It isn't me. The sound is still working fine."

Then it resumed. It sounded like Melship's voice.

'But how would we do this? Even as MPs we have limited powers...'

Lessiter commented, 'I'm not sure about this...It would be a significant betrayal of trust towards the electorate.'

'You forgot to say, 'financially rewarding',' said Mary Ranzino, 'With your new-found equity in Zillian, suitably placed offshore in a financial institution of your choosing, you can enjoy an oligarch's lifestyle. Once you have resigned from Parliament, of course.'

"FOBFO," said Clare. Christina and Bigsy giggled.

"Nah," said Jake, "You've got me again. I know FOMO - Fear of missing out, but not FOBFO."

"Fear of Being Found Out," chorused Christina and Clare.

"It's far more gangsta," added Bigsy.

Jake did a mock facepalm and groaned, "Children," he said, "I'm working with children."

The conversation from the conference room

continued.

'But how...would this work?' asked Melship.

"Hooked," observed Bigsy.

A two-stage thing

'It is a two-stage thing,' explained Miller McDonald.

'First, we launch Zillian, backed by Brant and touting its long -term credentials through the acquisition of Weide. The entire launch will be handled by Red Fox, as a form of insulation.'

McDonald continued, 'But here's the thing. We'll position the first customer deliveries of the $90,000 Zillian 502 sedan. It will be to a few people from the 'reserved list'. Celebrities and Instagram influencers posed next to one of the shiny new all-electric cars.

It will be just as the IPO goes live and we should get an immediate lift of at least 10% in the share price on the back of it. There will be a feeding frenzy as investors get into the share.

A week later, these same celebrities will announce that they can't believe the mileage they are getting from the vehicles. It is as if the vehicles recharge themselves whilst they are parked. Someone will announce that they have achieved over 450 miles between charges.'

"Impossible," said Bigsy, "Today's battery technology has finite limits."

Mary Ranzino continued, 'The effect of these quotes will be enough to see another rise of the share price. Maybe another 10 per cent.'

'That's when we announce the service vehicles,' explained McDonald. "It may be boring for the average car buyer, but we will announce a range of service vehicles. A van, a minibus, a delivery truck and a full-sized bus.'

Ranzino spoke again, "Maybe only a few points from this announcement, until the UK Government, via Douglas Melship, Secretary of State for Department for Transport Efficiency- DfTE announces it has decided to place a significant order for the UK. All government service vehicles to be provided on a rental agreement from Zillian. The projection of some 20,000 units should be enough to boost the price again."

'And then, a further piece of policy work. I had it prepared, and it will unfold through an announcement by Douglas Lessiter Minister of State for Infrastructure.

They could hear paper rustling and then Mary Ranzino spoke again.

'Here we are:'

'The UK must move away from "20th century thinking centred around private vehicle ownership" and towards shared mobility, Minister of State for Infrastructure, Douglas Lessiter has said.

'Lessiter said that shared mobility must become "the norm" as he outlined support for a future transport system which, he claimed, would introduce "greater flexibility, with personal choice and low carbon shared transport."

'Addressing this week's Collaborative Mobility Conference (CoMoUK), the Infrastructure Minister said it was "staggering" that nearly two-thirds of car trips are taken by lone drivers, and said the UK is at a "tipping point" where shared mobility will soon be a "realistic option for many of us to get around."

'As many industry analysts speculate whether Original Equipment Manufacturers (OEMs) will ever return to the pre-COVID new car registrations highs, a vision of a new transport system where Mobility Hubs become a familiar part of our street architecture, and where all these options will be available to book and pay for at the touch of a smartphone was shared with conference delegates.

'Furthermore, I am announcing the Framework legislation to support these vital changes to the UK's infrastructure, starting with London, in Parliament in the current term. It is a vital element required to meet the Government targets of carbon reduction.'

Mary Ranzino paused, and those in Christina's room realised that it was to give Lessiter and Melship a chance to think.

'That's another boost in share price and politically very enticing for the UK Government who can show they can move faster than the EU or the United States. The shaky Prime Minister will be delighted to have something positive to talk about and it can only do the Zillian share price further good.'

'But how will we get our initial allocations of equity?" asked Melship.

'This is where it becomes a win-win,' said Valeryevich. 'We will take care of your initial stake holding. In fact, we have already done so. My friends from Moscow have already donated £1 million to a private account for each of you, with Bank Rossiya, in Cyprus.'

"Bank Rossiya in Cyprus!" said Christina," I think that has fallen out of favour with Russian Mafia nowadays - it was linked to Putin via Sergei Roldugin and Yuri Kovalchuk - a couple of his close friends who are uncovered in the Panama Papers scandal. I think we might need Amanda Miller's help if we want to dig any further into this."

"What about if they are smart? If the Russians are working with the Chinese but don't want to give too much away?" asked Jake.

Christina agreed, "Sure, that could be grounds for using some questionable mechanisms in the set-up."

Melship again, 'But how do we gain access?'

Valeryevich, 'You don't, at least not for a while.'

Ranzino, 'You will be able to watch the money as it gets invested into Zillian and grows.'

Valeryevich, 'We are using investments like yours to help seed the growth of Zillian. You will be early purchasers of the Zillian launch and ride the shares all the way up.'

"It's a classic semi-state model," said Christina, "Just the usual Russian game play when they were selling off the State's equities. They sold the banks to their friends and then lent money to one-another to buy other state enterprises at knock-down prices. This is just a variation of the old ways."

"But will the owners get thrown out of tall buildings at the end?" asked Jake.

"Leverage," explained Christina, "Play along and Lessiter and Melship should become very rich very quickly."

"And if they don't?" asked Bigsy.

"Then I'm afraid they would be following Isabella," said Christina.

Sleaze

Gangsta rap

The meeting had ended and there were sounds of scraping chairs from the conference room.

"Stay away," said Christina, "We'll wait for Hannah and Lottie to return. They did well with their microphones. Thank you, also, Bigsy."

"They have some bottle," said Bigsy, "I'm not sure I could have sat through that whole session like that."

Christina's suite's doorbell rang. She walked over to answer it.

Hannah and Lottie walked in.

"My god!" said Hannah, "That was the scariest thing I've ever done! In a room full of global gangsters! When we left, we took a very roundabout route to get here, to ensure we were not followed."

Christina looked at them both and gestured to them to remain silent.

"Bigsy, can you check them for bugs? I'm thinking about countermeasures."

Bigsy retrieved a small orange device from his bag and approached Lottie.

"Ahem, I hope you won't mind?" he asked as he swept Lottie first and then Hannah for electronics, with the small device with what looked like a tape measure made into a 40 centimetre 'U' shaped aerial. He found their phones and his own microphones, but nothing else.

"All clear," he declared.

"Clare, your friends - the adventures - I said it just keeps on giving!" declared Lottie. She eyed the minibar in the room.

"Oh, please, help yourself," said Christina, "You've earned it! I'll call for some drinks to be delivered here."

Jake asked, "So what else did we discover? We could hear the voices but couldn't read the body language?"

"They all looked very serious. Melship seemed more compliant than Lessiter. I'm not even sure that Lessiter would go along with this if it wasn't for how deep he was already into everything," said Hannah.

"I could also see that Valeryevich was playing hard

ball, but he looked as if he was taking a lead from Qiu Zhang. She didn't say much, but I sensed she had the power in the room. What did you think, Lottie?"

"I agree, I had a feeling that the whole show was being put on for Qiu Zhang's sake. I could see several glances from everyone except Melship and Lessiter towards Qiu Zhang. I also couldn't stop noticing her clothes. She was by far the best dressed. I think her dress was Gucci, judging by the discreet brooch in a G shape on the shoulder. And she was so young! I'm guessing early thirties tops."

"Yes, and her arms were sculpted, like she was a fitness instructor," added Hannah.

"As I suspected, she's MSS, for sure," said Christina, "An agent of their Enterprises Division responsible for the operation and management of front companies, enterprises, and other institutions. She is tasked to help China get more control in the west and has the money to support these aims."

Jake looked at his phone. "I've just had a message from Amanda. She wants an update. I'm guessing she must have someone else here. She seems very well informed."

"Shall we do it now, or do we need longer to consider things? " Asked Clare.

"I think we are good," said Jake, "And we can ask whether Grace has found out anything about Qiu Zhang and Volvakov Kirill Valeryevich as well."

Carrots and sticks

"Okay, I'll put the audio through the same set-up," said Bigsy, "Except this time I'll plug in the microphones so everyone here will be heard by Amanda."

Jake dialled Amanda and they waited patiently for her to answer.

"Hi Jake, thanks for getting back so quickly," came Amanda's voice. It sounded as if she was on a speakerphone too.

"Unusual with no video, nowadays," observed Jake.

"To you, maybe. We still use an awful lot of ATCs, Audio Teleconferences," replied Amanda, "Oh and as you can't see her, I should mention that Grace Fielding is here with me! She says hello to everyone."

"Well, here in Gstaad, they - Brant and friends - just finished their meeting with Zillian, the automotive manufacturer, " stated Jake, "Our general supposition was right. Brant/Zillian are trying to influence Douglas Lessiter and Duncan Melship. They want the MPs to help further the cause of Zillian. There are several stages, each of which is designed to boost the base share price of Zillian. This will be at least partly achieved by MP endorsements of Zillian and UK Government policy, and as a reward Melship and Lessiter are both to be given a stake holding in the company."

What sort of stake holding?" asked Amanda.

Jake explained, "Financial, in effect a shareholding. They are being given money, which each of them uses to buy initial shares in the company. Then they see the shares rise significantly in value because of their endorsements. The initial money is being held for each of them, in trust in an offshoot of Bank Rossiya in Cyprus."

"That's Putin's Bank," said Amanda, "I mean he is a major shareholder, said to be worth billions in holdings."

"Well, we thought Russia, but then we also have Qiu Zhang's involvement," added Christina.

"Qui Zhang - she's from MSS, isn't she?" asked Amanda, "So it's a China/Russia alliance at work here?"

"I wondered that as well," said Christina, "I've already set in motion some enquiries. My sense is that it is being bankrolled by the Chinese though. It reminds me of a Russian scheme, but from many years ago. I doubt whether the Kremlin would operate this way now, except if this was some kind of leveraged deal,"

"I wondered too," said Clare, "I mean, £1 million each sounds like a lot for these two MPs, but for a Russian state deal it would be like chicken-feed."

"Exactly," said Christina, "Although I suppose the Chinese are adding plenty to the pot, if they want to quietly assume control of Zillian."

"China already owns several European automotive brands," said Grace, "Volvo was sold to Ford but then bought by China. Geely, I think. Then there was MG, saved by BMW but sold on and then picked up by Nanjing Auto, who in turn sold the brand to a Chinese State company. Pirelli tyres are majority owned by a Chinese chemical company and even Lotus is half Chinese and half Malaysian."

Clare summarised, "So what we get to, is two British MPs helping a scam to boost the share price of Zillian, where part of the funding is from China, but where Russia is still implicated?"

Christina nodded, "Yes, that is what it seems like, but I can't help wondering why Russia would nowadays be interested in such small fry numbers."

"I think the clue might be with Putin's Bank linkages," said Amanda, "That and the Chinese interest in the project."

"Clones!" said Bigsy suddenly, "If the Chinese want to learn how to copy things! This could be a test run by China, under Russia's tuition!"

Grace spoke, "Consider using legitimate companies as a money laundering system. It is already commonplace in Russia, but less so in China. Remember the Panama Papers?"

"Yes, I do," said Jake, "A network of secret offshore deals and loans worth $2bn which laid a trail to Russia's president, Vladimir Putin. The setup made members of Putin's close circle fabulously wealthy."

"That is right," said Grace, "Though the president's name does not appear in any of the records, the data reveals a pattern. His friends earned millions from deals that seemingly could not have been secured without his patronage. Furthermore, the documents suggested Putin's family has benefited from this money including massive unsecured loans to Sandalwood Continental, extending $650m in credit. Sandalwood was a reputed investment vehicle of Putin."

"I see, suddenly it's not a couple of million any longer," said Jake.

"And the laundering has been speculated to run into the billions," said Grace.

Amanda spoke, "This seemed to be the tip of an

iceberg. If Melship and Lessiter play along, then we'll have a worsening situation before we know it. Aside from the money, there must be another form of pressure operating. Carrot and Stick."

"Simple, old-fashioned sleaze," said Christina, "These two boys have been in Geneva and Gstaad for almost a week. They have barely attended any of the Car Expo meetings, instead sending along Lottie and Hannah. They have been out to play, under the guidance of Bérénice Charbonnier, who knows how things go down in Geneva and Gstaad - all the way from Rue Docteur-Alfred-Vincent to Rue du jeu de l'Arc."

Bigsy looked a little surprised that Christina knew so much about Geneva.

"Remember, Bigsy, I've been here before," added Christina, noticing Bigsy's expression.

"So, it really is carrot and stick?" asked Jake, "To Amanda's point, they get money and shares as their carrot, and sleazy smears as the stick."

Pressure Point

"We will need to tempt them to break cover," suggested Jake.

"Or to lean on Melship and Lessiter?" added Bigsy.

"Yes, and I think we have a pressure point," said Christina, "Remember that Lessiter was trying to stop Isabella Stevens before she was found in the river? - I'm sorry, Hannah, to bring this up."

Hannah nodded, "Yes, but I want to find her killers, too; she was a lovely person."

"Well, it may lead to a method to scare Lessiter," said Christina. "We know that Isabella had signed an NDA. The Non-Disclosure Agreement. Now we need to persuade Lessiter that Isabella let something slip. Something that he could also have let slip. It could be a way to rattle him. Particularly if he thinks it was his fault that Isabella was killed."

"But do we know what was in the NDA?" asked

Jake.

"I'm guessing it is very similar to the one that I had to sign," said Hannah, "I'll need to find a copy of it on my laptop, I can send it to you all."

"Amanda, what do you think of the plan? I know it is somewhat tactical," Christina asked.

"You are using the available assets wisely," said Amanda, "And some of them won't automatically be suspected of SI6 links either. I'm sure Qiu Zhang won't have realised that Hannah and Lottie are linked into SI6. It makes this a good plan to exert pressure."

Hannah's disappearance

"Last day today!" said Jake, "Then tomorrow we're back to London. I shall miss the walk from the chalet to the hotel!"

He had just appeared at the hotel's breakfast table, where Lottie and Clare were seated.

"Where is Hannah?" he asked, looking around, "Ah, I know, with her good friend Tony!"

"Not this time," answered Lottie, "As a matter of fact, Tony was here earlier and asking if any of us had seen her. He said he could not reach her on his phone, either."

"Yes, so I tried," said Lottie, "You know, in case there was a reason that Hannah didn't want to pick up for Tony, but no, nothing. It wasn't even going through to voicemail."

"Oh, she must be with Lessiter, then. He probably wants to demand a report from her."

"You might have thought so, but Lessiter also called me to ask of Lottie's whereabouts," answered Lottie.

"After that I decided to let myself into her room - Allegra opened her room for me. It didn't look as if she'd even been back to the chalet," answered Lottie.

"Oh, well that paints a different picture!" said Clare suddenly looking agitated, " I think she may well be missing."

Those around the breakfast table looked at one another, "Are we overreacting?" asked Jake, "I mean she could be -er - with someone?"

"Not Hannah," said Lottie, "Well, if she was, she'd have told me, at least, as a principle of security."

At that moment Christina and Bigsy arrived, "Why the glum faces?" Christina asked, looking around.

"We think Hannah has gone missing," explained Jake.

"I might be able to help with her whereabouts," said Bigsy," I wasn't going to tell any of you, but I added trackers to your jackets, back at the chalet."

"Bigsy?" said Clare, looking aghast, "You've been stalking us all?"

"Well, not exactly, but I realised that we could need to keep tabs one another over here. The ski jackets seemed like the most obvious piece of kit that would be taken everywhere."

"Well, it seems like a good idea now," said Christina, "How quickly can you run a trace, and how accurate is it?"

"I can do it from my laptop and it should be accurate to within a few metres, the tags auto-connect to any nearby phone to relay back their position, using the GPS from the phone. It is a pretty basic system, yet surprisingly effective."

"But why would Hannah want to disappear, or who would want to abduct her?" asked Clare.

"I think there's numerous suspects based upon what we know now, centred around what she knows about Lessiter's plans, and even that NDA she has on her laptop," answered Jake.

"Did anyone receive it yesterday?" asked Clare, "I know I didn't, but I put it down to the late hour."

She looked around the table and could see shaking heads.

"It could be the trigger for her being lifted," said Christina, "To stop us from seeing the Non-Disclosure Agreement. If it is the same as the one that Isabella had signed, then Lessiter seems to care greatly about its content."

"Now, an admission...We all enjoyed that ride in

Antanov's helicopter the other day. No-one asked why he'd brought such a large one along..."

"I did wonder," said Clare, "But it was incredibly useful."

"Well, it was fully loaded with passengers when it first arrived in Gstaad. He brought a squad of eleven soldiers with him, from the 76th Russian Airborne Division and led by a staff sergeant. These soldiers are all professionals and combat hardened. My Russian handler thought that I might need some backup."

"And why was that?" asked Jake.

"Blackbird had received further information. It suggested that the disruption being caused here in Gstaad were designed to lead back to the Kremlin. Blackbird had been told that the Kremlin was as much in the dark about this operation as everyone else."

"What, the Zillian scheme?" asked Bigsy.

"Correct, he said that it looked as if the scheme was designed to make the Kremlin look culpable. He hinted that it could expose some of Putin's own moves as well."

"So, any further idea who is driving this?" asked Clare, "Could it be the Chinese?"

"That's what Fyodor suggested," said Christina, "It

puts Volvakov Kirill Valeryevich under Qiu Zhang's control. He would be working for an agent of the Chinese MSS. And Miller McDonald and Mary Ranzino from Brant appear to be up to their usual tricks, too."

"But there are not so many Chinese/Russian gangsters, though?" queried Clare.

"If we look through post-Soviet gangsters, we find many nationalities," answered Christina, "Russian, Ashkenazi Jews, Estonian, Chechen, Tatar, Georgian, Armenian, Azerbaijani, but I've never seen a Chinese member operating inside the Russian Mafia, nor the Kremlin."

"But could it be the other way around?" asked Clare.

"The Honghuzi?" asked Christina, "They were sometimes called 'The Brothers', but they were silenced by the end of the 1940s. I don't think they have anything to do with 'The Brothers Circle' in Moscow."

"No," said Clare, "I think it is what Blackbird suggested. That the exposure of the Zillian moves could inadvertently lead back to the way that the Russian Central Bank has handled money on behalf of Putin."

Christina continued, "RCB/Sberbank is vast, with sometimes a reported 80,000 branches and numerous spin-offs. They say a close friend of Putin runs the bank nowadays. Add that to Putin's reputed net worth of between $70 and $200 billion and you can see why he won't want anyone looking around his arrangements too closely."

"No wonder they wanted to silence Isabella, and threaten Lessiter," said Bigsy, "Look, I've managed to run that trace. It looks as if Hannah is still here in Gstaad. They must want to use her to threaten Lessiter. They obviously don't think that Hannah knows anything."

"So that means the threat to Lessiter using Hannah only lasts as long as they are both here in Gstaad," said Christina.

Bigsy tuned his laptop and pointed to an area on the map. Clare asked him, "That is in the mountains, it looks close to the cable car stop?"

"Yes, it looks like a machinery depot, where they keep the snow ploughs. But it also has a brilliant outlook." Bigsy switched to a Street View image around the building.

"Look, see, it has a well-fortified position, but there is a fast and wide ski-run that passes almost next to it."

"Yes, I can see it has defence, yet good access as well," said Christina.

"However, we can show this to Antanov and I'm sure he, with an Mi-171, and eleven from 76th Airborne Division can handle Hannah's rescue," said Christina.

"Do we need to tell Amanda?" asked Jake.

"Afterwards, I suggest," said Christina, "Never ask permission from someone with a power of veto, if you are sure it is the right thing to do."

Jake grinned.

Second Order thinking

"But wait," says Clare, "What happens afterwards? If we rescue Hannah? I mean - the consequences?"

"Let's think about it for a moment," says Christina, "We'll be successful, of that, I am sure."

"Right, " says Clare, " So we rescue Hannah and bring her back in the helicopter."

"There will be prisoners too," says Jake, "I don't know how many, but they will be some kind of mercenaries."

"So, we could bring them back on the same helicopter," answers Christina, "It is the simplest thing to do."

"And where do we put them? We now have prisoners," says Jake.

"Misdirection," says Christina, "We must make them think we are from another force."

"Okay, but what kind of force?" asks Jake.

"We can imply the Russian bratva network," says Christina, "That's the organised crime network in Russia. No-one will want to mess with that. And I think we should use a gang like Solntsevskaya to create the impression that we are somehow linked to one of Russia's major transnational criminal organisations -- Vory v Zakone or "ladrones de la ley" - the thieves in law.

"Solntsevskaya has well-documented linkages with Mexican criminal organisations. They ship drugs like cocaine, heroin, and methamphetamines to resorts, hotels or houses protected and owned by their Mexican associates."

"I see," says Clare, "We make it look as if they have moved Hannah to a hideout that somehow crosses a Solntsevskaya line. That they are angry and want to sound a warning shot to move the trespassers out of town."

"Perfect," says Bigsy.

"Just a little complicated, " says Jake.

"So, what do we do with the prisoners?" asks Clare.

"We put them on a plane from Geneva to Juarez," answers Christina, "It's around 20 hours with a Moscow stopover. I can get that authorised through Blackbird. We can turn them loose in Mexico City and let them fend for themselves. If they have any sense they will go to ground, because they will be worried that they are being hunted. And no-one from around here will believe that it isn't a put-up job - In other words that they were paid to let Hannah escape."

"Wow!" says Lottie, "You guys don't mess around! But what about the protection for Hannah?"

"We'll make it known to our charming little gang from Zillian, that Hannah is now under Bratva protection. That can be easily achieved via a few well-placed emails and texts," explained Christina.

"Then, I assume it becomes business as usual?" asks Jake.

"Correct," says Christina, "Although I think Lessiter will be abnormally worried by this turn of events."

"Yes, if one assistant died and another goes missing from his team, it would be sufficient grounds for a full-blown investigation of him," says Jake.

"Yes, although if we do this right, Hannah should be able to return her role without a fear of further reprisals. The time is almost up." answers Christina.

"And, assuming this all works, we are all out of here tomorrow!" says Jake.

Small airstrip, big helicopter

Bigsy drove them in a minibus to a small airstrip on the outskirts of Gstaad. A separate military truck was parked adjacent to what Clare thought of as Antanov's helicopter. Clare watched the helicopter load up with the selected members of Russia's 76th Airborne. She was not going on this flight, although Antanov and Christina were piloting the large helicopter. If everything ran to plan, they would be back within an hour.

Bigsy, Jake and Lottie stood by her side, all of them watching the small mix of tough-looking men and women in black combat gear climb into the helicopter.

Then, the rotors started and the noisy 'copter took to the sky. Soon they could only hear the rotor beats and then what they assumed was the sound of the helicopter descending towards the target building. In the expanse of the valley, it was unlikely that anyone else would even notice the sounds.

Ten minutes later, they could hear the helicopter starting up once more and then, an increasingly loud sound as they could eventually see its three front lights, red, green, and white, as it once more approached the landing strip.

A flurry of snow, and the helicopter landed, further away this time and close to a coach with boarded side windows. They watched, as first the soldiers and then four figures disembarked and they could see what looked like two men and two women herded toward the coach.

A heavy motor started and it was on its way, followed by the original military truck that the soldiers had been delivered in. A smaller group led by Christina crunched over toward them in their cold huddle. Then a single figure broke and ran toward them. Hannah.

"My god!" she called, "Am I glad to see all of you!"

"Okay, let's sit in the bus and you can tell us all what happened," said Jake, gesturing to the nearby parked VW-Transporter. As Christina climbed aboard, he noticed her wink at him.

Suspicion-less

They were all the minibus, with Hannah in the front seat, next to Bigsy, who prepared to drive them back to the chalet.

"So, what happened?" asked Lottie, as Bigsy started the engine.

Hannah began, "It was intense, but also like a dream. A female police officer came to find me during the conference. She had I.D. and said that she needed to take me to Lessiter. That something had happened to Lessiter and he had asked for me. She showed me to a police car, a regular white and orange Hyundai, which had 'Polizei' in big letters on the side - oh, and a blue roof light."

"You weren't suspicious?" asked Lottie.

"Oh, no, I thought that Lessiter had got himself into some bother, maybe something that would require him to be extracted from a jail or something. Anyway, I got into the back of the car and the policewoman sat next to me. There were two heavy set men in the front, although they looked like plain clothes detectives or something."

"Where did this happen?" asked Christina.

Hannah began, "Right outside the Expo, the car was almost at the main entrance...Well, they drove me for what seemed like a long time and I realised we were heading out of town. It was quiet in the car as well; they didn't seem to have radios bleeping or anything like you see in regular cop shows on TV."

"Then they took a turning and the car climbed a way toward the place where they eventually held me. I thought that Lessiter must have been there, maybe with some form of entertainment. I assumed the police were keeping it low-key, maybe to avoid diplomatic embarrassment.

Hannah looked around at the group. Everyone was leaning in, listening to the story, except Bigsy, who was concentrating on driving.

"They showed me into a very modern-looking building, like an architect-designed house, about 5 kilometres from Gstaad, I'd guess. It was on a slope and near to a cable-car."

"That'll be around Videmanette, close to where we landed the helicopter when we came to find you. It's actually about 14 kilometres from Gstaad!" said Christina.

"That's when the policewoman said that they would be grateful for my co-operation, and could I hand over my phone. Now I was suspicious and then another policewoman appeared from one of the rooms of the house."

"Did you notice another police car?" asked Christina.

"No, but I asked what the hell was happening; to be truthful I had no idea. The second police officer asked me to sit down, that they had something important to say."

Bigsy was indicating to turn into the main streets of Gstaad, "Maybe you should move to a less visible seat," said Christina, "Here swap with me."

Hannah and Christina swapped seats and Hannah continued, "Then they explained to me that I was being held, pending deportation. That Lessiter had been involved in a club scandal and that the decision was to simply deport his entire party, to move the problem away. To be truthful, it all seemed kind of believable. Then the first woman told me I was technically being held by Bern Canton, but that they would treat me respectfully so long as I didn't try anything."

Jake asked, "So you were held, in custody, in a safe house?"

"That's what I thought. I could not believe that this was happening. I said I needed to make a phone call, but they said it was not allowed, neither was I to have any form of solicitor privilege. I asked why they were not holding me in the police facility and was told for diplomatic reasons I had been taken to a *sicheres Gebäude* - a safe building - outside of Gstaad to reduce the chance of adverse publicity, particularly involving Lessiter and the Car Expo. It did all seem kind of plausible, what with Lessiter being an MP and these being police officers."

"But you didn't ask for any other form of I.D?" asked Christina.

"No and given that they were in uniforms and I was transported by police car, I was believing them. I asked how long I would be detained, and they said it would be until my planned return to the UK-literally the next day."

"Didn't they offer to tell anyone of your whereabouts?" asked Bigsy.

"They said they would leave a message at the Expo that for diplomatic reasons I had been taken to police headquarters, but that they would ensure I was on the 'plane back to the U.K. I would not be allowed to contact anyone until I was back on the 'plane."

Bigsy was indicating to turn into the road to their chalet. They would be back in another minute. He could see in the distance that Allegra was moving some shopping from her car.

Hannah continued, "The two women spoke good English, but quite heavily accented. They were very kind to me. They said that as police officers there were certain parts of their jobs that they didn't like and this was one of them."

Bigsy switched off the engine, but everyone remained in the minibus.

"That evening, to disarm me even further, the two policewomen rustled up a delicious Tartiflette, with acres of Reblochon cheese."

"Tartiflette?" asked Bigsy.

"It's a combination of thinly sliced potatoes, smoky bits of bacon, caramelised onions and oozy, nutty, creamy Reblochon cheese," answered Lottie, "You missed our evening at Le Flore, in Geneva, Bigsy, when we had that huge round Tartiflette to share!"

"Don't keep reminding me about that evening when you all went out and left me charging gadget batteries!" answered Bigsy - he waved to Allegra from the front of the minibus, then held up a splayed hand as if to signal five minutes. Allegra did a 'thumbs up' in response.

"But you see my point?" asked Hannah, "I might have been held captive, but because they were not being all menacing with duct tape and ropes, and they were feeding me well, I thought it was a pleasurable way to spend about 30 hours in detention. I didn't even know I needed to be rescued by helicopter by a squad of Special Forces until it happened!"

Clare looked around the group. She could see that they were mainly smiling. But she knew it could have gone very differently.

"What has happened to the four of them?" asked Bigsy.

Christina answered, "Antanov has them detained now. They are all from a unit of GRU Spetznaz - that's the Russian Special force used to infiltrate other countries. I assumed they were being shipped back to Russia; if they stay in Switzerland there is a chance that they will cause problems."

"I assume travel is through your friend Blackbird?" asked Hannah, to Christina.

"Yes, although we are as confused as everyone about who is working for whom in all of this."

"And how much does Lessiter know?" asked Hannah, "Does he even know I'd been abducted?"

"Lessiter will know, " said Christina, "The whole point of them taking you is to show Lessiter that they can get at anyone, and any time."

Jake spoke, "So that will be the 'stick' part of the process. He gets a lot of money to assist but knows that if he doesn't then bad things can happen."

Clare added, "Now we must be careful about what we do over the next day. As we fly back tomorrow, we could keep Hannah hidden until the flight, to create the illusion that the plan has worked. Then I could ask Antanov and one of his Special Unit to accompany Hannah to the gangway to the plane. It could look quite theatrical, but should do the trick," said Christina.

"Could we have Hannah delivered to the steps onto the plane, " asked Jake.

"Yes, I'm sure we can arrange that, although we'll need a military vehicle to make it look right," answered Christina, "I expect Antanov will know where to get one."

"And Hannah's back-story?" asked Clare, "It can be almost how she described it, Lessiter won't want to contradict anything, because it can only dig him a deeper hole."

Christina continued, "The difference in the story can be that Hannah stayed in the 'safe house' until the flight. She was well-looked after but had been told Lessiter was at first detained but then released from police custody after a misunderstanding."

She continued, "Antanov found out that Lessiter had been disorderly in 'La Cage' - a gender-fluid club in Gstaad, where he was wearing a purple minidress, with a grey neck swag, black tights, and black silver-tipped platform shoes. He claimed to have been drugged and forced to wear the clothes."

Jake and Bigsy burst out laughing, "Why not make the whole thing improbable?" said Bigsy.

"No, it's a thing," said Clare. Christina and Lottie nodded.

"Yes, it's a part of the scene in London too," added Lottie. Hannah nodded her agreement, "A little too often with Duggie, to be frank, I'm amazed that he gets away with it, he's even hidden it from that reporter Rachel Crosby. She was close to finding out a month or two ago."

Jake and Clare remembered their conversation with Rachel, back at the Caffè Concerto, in London. The oblique reference to the 'Fleet's In!' painting, which Clare had subsequently googled and confirmed her suspicions.

"Okay, so what will we say in front of Allegra?" asked Jake.

Christina replied, "As little as possible. Today, we went sightseeing with Bigsy, in the Minibus, but it broke down. It was ironic, being in Gstaad for a Car Expo. The local TCS (Touring Club of Switzerland) were dispatched to rescue us but we gave them the wrong location and so we lost a couple of hours whilst they located us. It was a minor electrical fault and the man from the TCS fixed it."

"Well, that sounds mundane compared with what actually happened!" said Bigsy. They all climbed out of the minibus Transporter.

"Wow, you all look as if you have been through the wars!" exclaimed Allegra, "You know what, tonight is your last night, I'm making you something simple and typically Swiss. With lots of garlic and cheese! - It's Tartiflette."

They all looked at Bigsy.

Window dressing

Clare sat in a window seat on the return flight. She could see Lessiter and Melship further forward in the Business Class seats at the front of the plane. They appeared to have a row each, with a protection officer sitting discreetly on the other side of the plane in seats JKL.

Clare was surprised that the return flights were on a commercial carrier instead of in a private jet, but then she realised the MPs had been flown out, courtesy of a car industry supplier, but they had been forced to return under their own arrangements.

Clare remarked about this to Lottie.

Lottie answered, "It's window dressing - it looks far less privileged if they come back on their own pocket. Ever since that scandal about the Minister who flew from London to Australia on a private 220 seater A320 jet. It cost the Minister their chance of a run at the top job."

"Yes, I suppose there's those photographers who hang around at Heathrow too, looking out for celebrities and public figures."

Lottie nodded, "Any minute now it should get interesting, when Hannah gets on the plane!"

They could see a black SUV had driven to the left-hand side of the plane. Then she could see several military personnel and a woman - Hannah - climb out. Hannah was shown to a set of steps which wound their way onto the jetway and then they saw her appear at the front of the plane. She was rapidly shown to her seat, which Lottie and Clare noticed was in the same select area as the seats of Lessiter and Melship.

"Look. Lessiter looks surprised," whispered Clare, to Lottie.

"I can just make out what they are saying," said Lottie.

"It seems Lessiter had been told that Hannah had to return early, back to London. He does look surprised to see her here."

"He could have phoned her to check she was okay," answered Clare.

"That's why they have assistants like us - to do those kinds of calls," said Lottie, "Not that I'm bitter."

The rack above the seats made a 'bong' sound and the pre-flight announcements meant they were ready for take-off.

"Goodbye Geneva," said Clare.

"Goodbye Gstaad," echoed Lottie.

Intense

They were back in Heathrow, and Clare could see Lessiter agitatedly taking to Hannah. It reminded her of the scene back at the Christmas party with Isabella Stevens, except this time Lessiter was not grabbing Hannah.

"Whoa! There's something intense going down between Lessiter and Hannah," said Jake. "And look, Melship is talking to Lottie."

Bigsy commented, "It is as if, now they are back in the UK, the two MPs have suddenly remembered that they have assistants. I expect hey are both setting up all the errands they want performed, so that both MPs can go home for a well-deserved rest."

Christina walked over, "It all seems to be resetting. By now Lessiter will have told Hannah that he thought she had to return early. That is why he did not miss her. And Melship will be unloading a range of errands for Lottie."

"Where is Antanov?" asked Jake.

"Oh, he had to escort the four captives back to Moscow," answered Christina.

"And what about Kjeld Nikolajsen, Miller McDonald and Mary Ranzino from Brant and Qiu Zhang and Valeryevich?" asked Jake

"We checked and Nikolajsen and McDonald have flown back to Norway, and Mary Ranzino and Qiu Zhang boarded a flight to Paris, whereas Valeryevich was heading for Moscow," answered Christina, "It was helpful having those Special Forces that Antanov brought."

"Paris seems like a random choice?" said Bigsy.

"Not really, it's a major hub to link with just about any major capital," replied Christina, "Ranzino still lives in New York, for example."

"What about us?" said Clare, "Is there anyone following us at the moment?" she looked at Christina.

"No, I don't think so," said Christina, "Anyway, they already know where each of us lives - or at least where we work,"

"How reassuring," muttered Clare.

Brading's Office

Monday, and everyone was back at work. Clare was in Parliament and back in Andrew Brading's office with Serena and Maggie.

"How did it go?" asked Serena, looking interested, "Did you find out anything fascinating about Duggie and Duncan?"

Maggie looked around, also interested in what Clare was going to say.

"Oh yes, they certainly both know how to freeload. It goes no further but poor Hannah and Lottie were dumped with all the work, whilst Duggie and Duncan were able to visit high-end entertainment in both Geneva and Gstaad."

"You don't surprise me," said Maggie, "There's still a great sense of entitlement with some of the MPs. We all know which Etonian occupant of Number 10 set the tone, and even with some casualties in the fall-out, there are still MPs who will continue to operate from a haughty sense of privilege."

Serena nodded, "Yes, Clare, you've seen your share of such MPs, from when you were here the last time as well. Don't get me wrong, there are some fine upstanding MPs, but there are also both likeable rogues and out-and-out scoundrels."

"Some of them simply fall into the wrong company," said Maggie.

"And others were born this way?" asked Clare.

"But let's face it, I'm not sure how much your time in Switzerland will have helped Andrew," observed Serena, "Have you anything for the Secretary of State for Internal Affairs?"

"We'll, as a matter of fact, I have, " answered Clare, " It looks as if a variation on the Minerva and Medusa scam is being run by an as-yet unknown power."

"Not more bribery and corruption of MPs?" asked Serena.

"I'm afraid so, and both Douglas Lessiter and Duncan Melship seem to be involved."

"Can this go public?" asked Serena, "Is there enough proof?"

"I'm afraid not. Both behaved badly whilst abroad, treating the trip like a 'jolly' but I think we've a developing situation because of some of the people they spoke to."

"Do Lottie Davis and Hannah know about it?" asked Serena.

"Yes, Hannah accompanied Douglas Lessiter and Lottie was with Duncan Melship. Figuratively speaking..."

"No great surprise if Melship was doing the round of the parties. I imagine he threw himself at every opportunity!" said Screna.

"And I imagine Douglas was - er - more selective about the company he kept?" asked Maggie.

"Well observed, Maggie, although Lessiter was also drinking the Kool-Aid. We, on the other hand were learning all about tyre pressures and the five stages of self-drive car evolution. And I can bore for Britain on battery life expectancy - Oh for a full electric car, the bottom line is about 100,000 miles, by the way."

"But as importantly, did you keep an eye on our two MPs?" asked Serena, "Amanda Miller impressed upon me the importance of that aspect of the visit. You are something of a dark horse, Ms Crafts!" Serena smiled at Clare.

Clare was relieved that Serena was prepared to be complicit in the plans briefed by Amanda.

"We're into Official Secrets Act territory now," explained Clare.

"The daring duo are mixed up in a car floatation share price scam," explained Clare, "It could make them both very rich, but I think whoever is running them has something over each of them too."

"Do we know who it is?" asked Serena, "I mean is it - er- individuals or a state action?"

"We don't know, the mix of people includes Americans, Chinese and Russians and there are also different companies in the background."

"I assume you'll be making a report to Amanda Miller?" asked Serena.

Clare nodded, "Yes, actually we were planning to do that today, later"

At that moment Andrew Brading appeared, "Oh, welcome back Clare! Look I am so sorry to be a bearer of some terrible news. Douglas Lessiter was involved in a road traffic accident. Very close to his London apartment. They say he died instantly."

"Oh my god," said Serena, "What happened?"

"A couple of witnesses said he was walking, weaving across the road, looking drunk and then he stepped out in front of a van. It ran straight over him and just kept on going - a hit and run. Apparently, the witnesses were quite shocked but one of them managed to write down the middle part of the van's registration. They didn't get it all and so far, the police can't get a good match on anything. It is supposed to be a white van. I can't imagine the driver will get far, with all the cameras in central London."

"Clare - you look pretty shaken," said Maggie.

"It is the last thing I would have expected!" answered Clare, "I mean, Lessiter seemed to be on the side of the whoever is plotting most of this."

Andrew Brading raised an eyebrow, "What's this? Was Lessiter mixed up in something? And was it with Melship?"

"I was explaining to Serena, it is similar to the previous corruption, with MPs being put on the hook and then offered enticements to do things to line the pockets of others."

"But there isn't sufficient proof," said Serena, "It is mainly supposition. You know what enquiries into MP behaviour can be like. And it has got worse since that shambolic charlatan duped everyone in Parliament."

Brading answered, "Yes, it has made it devilishly difficult for everyone honest since that last pack of lies and corruption was uncovered. It was as if it was all a part of the plan to make investigations of Parliament more convoluted."

"Okay, but what about Hannah? She was working with Lessiter and had a spare room at his apartment?" asked Clare.

"Oh? I didn't know that," said Serena. Andrew Brading also shook his head, but she noticed that Maggie remained quiet.

Clare added, "Yes, Lessiter provided Hannah with some digs in London. It suited him too and provided cover for his unusual predilections. It was all kept out of the press, although some of them knew or guessed," said Clare.

She noticed Maggie nodded at this.

"Are you and Hannah good friends?" asked Clare.

"Yes, we have known each other for several years. I've even been to visit her at Lessiter's place," added Maggie, "But it seemed to be - you know- private and personal. But right now, I wouldn't want anything to happen to Hannah."

"As a matter of fact, something happened in Gstaad," said Clare, "We are still speaking confidentially? Yes?"

"Agreed," said Serena.

"Hannah was abducted as part of a threat to Lessiter. We had to mount a full-blown rescue party to get Hannah back. However, the kidnappers were very refined and Hannah didn't even think she had been abducted. The kidnappers posed as policemen and she thought she was being detained in a safe house."

"So how on earth did you get her back?" asked Andrew.

"Well, remember my friends? A few of them assisted liberate Hannah from capture. There's a longer version of the story, but now is not the time," answered Clare. She thought it better not to mention the helicopter and the Russian Special Forces.

"You lead a very interesting life," observed Brading.

"Well, right now I think we should move Hannah to somewhere safe and secure," said Clare, "and that doesn't sound as if it should be Lessiter's spare room."

Maggie picked up her phone, "I'm calling Hannah. I'll ask her to come to this office. I'll say it's urgent. She should be on the Estate, somewhere."

"I'll authorise you to use one of the secure meeting rooms in Portcullis House. I'm assuming you'll want to bring in Amanda Miller?" said Andrew, "But you'll forgive me if I don't join you, I have another pressing matter at hand, and I'd really appreciate it if Maggie - at least - could join me."

Clare made a few phone calls, she would bring Jake, Bigsy, Lottie and Hannah to the session, as well as Christina.

Portcullis House

Clare started the walk across to Portcullis House. It passed along a few twisted corridors, with strategically placed buckets to collect rainwater. The Palace of Westminster building was still in need of some repairs. By comparison, Portcullis House was modern, with a swooping glass canopy over the atrium-like central space. Its site was once occupied by houses from the 1400s built for the dean and twelve canons of St Stephen's College at the Palace of Westminster. Much later it became the St. Stephen's Club. Underground, the District and Circle lines bisected the site and formed a deep well between the buildings, at the bottom of which was situated the deep tunnels of the Westminster underground station.

After the passing of the London Underground Act, it was deemed necessary to clear the whole corner site to build the new Jubilee Line station. This conveniently opened the possibility of a substantial new, freestanding building and the creation of a secure parliamentary campus extending as far as

Parliament Street and Richmond Terrace.

Sure enough, everyone was waiting for Clare in the visitor's lobby of Portcullis House. Hannah and Lottie have walked across from inside the Parliamentary complex."

"Jake and I came by taxi," explained Jake, "This sounded quite urgent. Although Christina wasn't with us, I expect she'll arrive by helicopter in a moment!"

They laughed, just as Christina made her way in, smiling "No helicopter, just a London cab!"

On this occasion, Clare was leading the group to Andrew's go-to meeting room in the complex. It was one of the more prestigious and secure rooms and illustrated that Andrew had clout as a Minister. They passed a scurrying weaselly 'Pomp' on the way to this session, but this Minister looked blankly ahead as if he was some absent-minded university Professor. It was a long-cultivated look, which he wrongly thought played well to television viewers.

"Bleurgh," whispered Bigsy, "I hate that man."

The others nodded in silent agreement.

"Ever since his back-stabbing play to depose the Prime Minister, he's been the enemy at one's back. As Andrew puts it: 'Remember, the opposition is in front of you; your enemy is behind you in your own party.'

"Oh dear," said Clare, "Another case of only the paranoid survive!"

Clare swiped her access card and they all trooped into the conference room.

"Nice," breathed Bigsy, "Although not quite as fancy as some of those along at SI6."

He pulled a small orange scanner from his bag and proceeded to sweep the room as if looking for surveillance equipment.

"They've done a good job here, not a bug in sight, " he muttered.

"Has someone already contacted Amanda?" asked Clare, suddenly realising that this ad-hoc session might be in vain.

"I'm ahead of you," said Jake, "We've got it set for 11am. In twenty minutes, with Amanda and Grace."

Hannah stared at Clare, "You had something important to tell me?" she asked, "What was it?"

"Oh Hannah, I guess you still haven't heard. I got the news from Andrew Brading. There's no easy way to tell you this. Duggie died this morning in a road accident."

They all looked at Hannah, whose face broke and she moved her hands to brush away slight tears.

"I knew something like this was on the cards, " she said, "Duggie was playing with fire. It's what Isabella was trying to warn him about."

Clare softly took Hannah's hand, "How could you be expecting this?" she asked.

Hannah straightened herself in the chair and put on her best serious Nicole Kidman expression.

"Look you must all know that I've been living in a room in his London apartment. It's purely platonic and came about when we both realised it was taking me too long to get to work. About 90 minutes each way, from deepest Hampshire. Duggie offered me his spare room, and by then, he had shared with me that he was gay - something I'd already worked out. Although he had not 'come out' in the conventional sense and was worried about his electorate's take if he were to suddenly announce it."

"The press were on to him as well," said Lottie, "That Rachel Crosby seemed to know."

"Yes, and actually she came around once to ask Duggie some questions. He asked me if I'd mind being around to provide a bit of camouflage. Of course, I didn't mind - and we'd become quite professionally close over the time that I worked for him."

Hannah continued, "I could see that Rachel was no fool and had scoped Duggie in the first few minutes.

I was trying to cut short her interview with him."

"But how did you know about whatever else Lessiter was doing?" asked Jake.

"He wasn't always that subtle. Izzy had spotted that he was being trapped into a paid lobbying situation and that was when he got all serious about the Non-Disclosure Agreements. To be frank, I think it was Brant that insisted upon them. I have one too."

"So, what happened?" asked Bigsy.

"Izzy wanted to warn Duggie that he was getting in too deep. That Brant was not an organisation to be messed with. If he wasn't careful, he could lose everything. She told me she was going to say it all to Duggie and I guess that as what was happening at that Xmas party,"

"I see, so she warns Lessiter not to be a fool?" asked Jake.

"Yes, but I think she must have threatened to be a whistle-blower too. That would have riled Duggie and been the reason he brought up the NDA."

"But it doesn't explain why she was in the Thames," said Lottie.

"My guess," said Christina, "Lessiter told someone that Isabella was a potential whistle-blower, and they clumsily dealt with her."

"Terrible, but who would it be?" asked Jake.

"It has to be someone involved with the Zillian scheme," said Christina, "And probably from Brant. They have access to all kinds of military contractors."

At that moment, there was a chiming sound in the room, and Clare pushed a button to reveal that Amanda and Grace had now joined the call.

"Hi Amanda, Hi Grace, " said Clare.

"Hello everyone," said Amanda, "And how are things?"

Clare began to summarise everything for Amanda, with additional inputs chipped in from everyone else.

Grace then flicked up a single chart. "So, this seems to be the story?"

LESSITER
- Hannah and Isabella work for Lessiter, both sign NDA
- Isabella discovers Lessiter is potentially compromised
- Isabella confronts Lessiter and threatens to whistle-blow.
- Isabella found in the Thames.

LESSITER AND MELSHIP

- Lessiter and Melship both have influence in transport lobby
- Both taken to Switzerland for Expo briefing
- Both wined, dined and 'befriended'.

BRANT ZILLIAN

- Melship and Lessiter propositioned for Brant/Zillian launch
- They are asked to assist in lobbying
- Both stand to make much money if they do as told.
- Hannah gets abducted, as leverage on Lessiter
- Hannah gets rescued, Lessiter told she is back in the UK.
- All return with apparently Lessiter and Melship prepared to do as told.
- Suspects include Bérénice Charbonnier, Kjeld Nikolajsen, Miller McDonald and Mary Ranzino from Brant and Qiu Zhang and Volvakov Valeryevich

IN UK

- Lessiter dies in Road Traffic Accident.
- Zillian scheme is poised to be executed
- Not clear, beyond Zillian and Brant,

who is running it.

"That is a good summary!" said Clare, enthusiastically.

"I can imagine Bérénice Charbonnier being mixed up in this, but not a ringleader, " said Christina.

"Kjeld is Norwegian and works for Brant, Miller and Mary are both Americans. Qui Zhang is Chinese and Valeryevich is Russian, so take your pick!" announced Bigsy.

"And The Kremlin is denying involvement," added Christina, "Although it doesn't rule it out, nor a bratva gang from Russia in charge."

"So, what are the next steps?" asked Clare.

There was a pause as everyone considered for a moment. It was Christina who spoke.

"I've been checking back, " she said, "Russia doesn't seem to know much about this. They know of the acts of Zillian, but don't seem to have anyone driving this."

"But can you be sure?" asked Amanda.

"Sure, in that my handler has asked me to look into it further. My handler supplied me with a helicopter, pilot and ten Special Force troops to go to Switzerland. I doubt very much whether I'd have got so much attention if the Kremlin new all about it."

"I can't speak directly to your handler, can I?" asked Amanda.

"No, it would be an embarrassing breach of protocol. I don't even think they know I have these occasional conversations with you," answered Christina.

"I have an evolving theory," said Grace, "Start by following the money. Who gains from all of this?"

"Melship and so would have Lessiter," said Clare.

"Yes, but who puts up most of the stake-holding?" asked Grace, "The Chinese. This could be a copycat situation. China is trying to do what the Russians did so successfully in the late 1990s. They can see that investing in the right enterprises could yield them millions."

"They could make money two ways, actually," observed Christina, "First through a share price rise and secondly by sourcing the actual Zillian vehicles in China."

"It could also create a massive money laundering vehicle for Russia," said Grace, "Think about it. It's a win-win for both China and Russia."

"It's like the old schemes we uncovered," said Jake, "Right back when they were operating the so-called green-lanes scams. It is, if you think about it, - ahem

- how The Triangle was formed."

"Yes, but I am sure that you only grabbed some passing 'small change'," said Grace, "In the Russian Federation, the estimates of capital flight frequently serve as a basis for money - laundering estimates because a significant part of the capital flight is presumed to be laundered illicit proceeds. The magnitude of capital flight itself causes suspicions about money-laundering."

"Capital Flight," smiled Bigsy, "I like it! A euphemism for stolen money!"

Grace continued, "In the 1990s, the magnitude of capital flight from the Russian Federation was significant. This was acknowledged by many sources, although there is no consensus about its nature and size.

"A joint project on capital flight undertaken by the Institute of Economics based in Moscow concluded that the average of different agencies' estimates equals a total of $133 billion for the period 1992-1997. Capital flight in the Russian Federation was running at an annual $17 billion. Then, in 1999 the Central Bank of the Russian Federation estimated the size of capital flight to be $54.2 billion for the period 1994-1998, which suggests an annual flow of about $11 billion."

"But hold it," said Clare, "Isn't that the same bank that is now wrapped up in this whole business?"

"It is," said Grace," and many say Putin himself has much equity with the bank. Ad indeed with many of the schemes, which required his sponsorship. They had built a money filtering factory, which was even up-front about the amount of money leaking from the system!"

"Hiding in plain sight!" said Christina.

Grace continued, "It is reasonable to assume that the capital leaving the Russian Federation illegally might be returning to the country disguised as legitimate foreign investment. The relationship between capital flight and foreign direct investment (FDI) appears to be clear-cut."

Christina spoke, "Yes don't you all see? This mechanism for creating huge wealth has been tested by the Russian Federation. Now they are branching out, using foreign companies and foreign investment to disguise what they are doing."

Christina continued, "Few in the Russian Federation worry about money laundering, but many are concerned about the enormous illicit proceeds from the theft and embezzlement of public and private assets. This concern echoes an international perception of the Russian Federation as a source of illicit proceeds, rather than as a safekeeping haven."

Jake spoke, "It's as if they are using the mechanics of the state and the bulk of personal savings to hide the gangster-like quantities of money being laundered"

Grace added, "In an effort to circumvent the legalisation of illegal profits, the Russian authorities have been tightening controls, which have included measures halting financial liberalisation and installing foreign exchange controls. Ironically, China is only just waking up to this."

Jake spoke, " I suppose the immense secrecy surrounding much of what goes on in China also acts a brake on new legislation?"

"Yes, you are kind-of right. You can't administer what you don't know about," said Grace.

"I remember something called S-Special accounts, in Russia," said Christina, "I used to get paid through them."

Grace nodded, "Exchange control mechanisms, including suspension of operations through non-residents, so-called "S-special" accounts, were introduced and prompted innovations circumventing these restrictions. The schemes involved foreign holders of roubles and Russian companies interested in doing business with them. Under the scheme, the shares of the Russian companies sold for roubles to foreign companies were purchased back by the same Russian companies for hard currencies.

"I see, " said Jake, "A Magic Roundabout of money. Put something impure in, wait a while and out pops the equivalent legitimate money."

"Correct," said Grace, "To purchase the shares, the Russian companies use their foreign currency holdings abroad. Zillian would be a good example. The Russian authorities described these operations as of a limited scale and not of a criminal nature. Nevertheless, they raise questions about why and how Russian companies have been able to accumulate and keep abroad assets of such size."

"They started this a long time ago," said Christina, "The sell-off of Russian banks and then state companies using the banks to pay for the shares in the companies, then seeing everything rise in value, so the original bank loans could easily be repaid. A popular Russian pun equates privatisation to the grabbing of State assets. Privatisation is referred to as prihvatization. 'Hvatat' in Russian means to grab, which could be also understood as a robbery."

"Wow, and I assume everyone got rich?" asked Jake.

"Yes, rich or murdered," answered Christina, "Many were killed as the next wave of nouveau-capitalists appeared to take control."

"Hmm, I wonder if that is what we are seeing now with Lessiter meeting his end?" asked Jake.

China, my China

In the haze of the morning, China sits on eternity
And the opium farmers sell dreams to obscure fraternities
On the horizon the curtains are closing
Down in the orchard the aunties and uncles play their games
(like it seems they always have done)

In the blue distance the vertical offices bear their names
(like it seems they always have done)
Clocks ticking slowly, dividing the day up
These poor girls are such fun they know what God gave them
fingers for (to make percussion over solos)

China my china, I've wandered around and you're still here
(which I guess you should be proud of)
Your walls have enclosed you, have kept you at home for
thousands of years (but there's something I should tell you)
All the young boys are dressing like sailors

I remember a man who jumped out from a window over the bay
(there was hardly a raised eyebrow)
The coroner told me 'this kind of thing happens every day'
You see, from a pagoda, the world is so tidy.

Brian Eno

China

"We should talk about China," says Amanda, "Grace, what have you found?"

Grace begins, "As China's growing global role and increasingly hardline policies at home and abroad gain attention, the United States and other Western governments are also taking notice of China's expanding influence in developing countries."

"They should do, with the number of products now made in China," says Bigsy.

Grace continues, "The implications of China's growing investments linked to the Belt and Road Initiative (BRI) which is its global infrastructure and connectivity program, are increasingly debated. So, too, are the nature of Chinese Communist Party (CCP) efforts to popularize its authoritarian model and undermine developing democracies around the world, whether intentionally or indirectly."

Jake adds, "Belt and Road? The Belt is the 'Silk Road

Economic Belt' referring to the proposed overland routes for road and rail transportation through landlocked Central Asia along the famed historical trade routes of the Western Regions. I remember 'Road' is short for the '21st Century Maritime Silk Road', referring to the Indo-Pacific Sea routes through Southeast Asia to South Asia, the Middle East and Africa. Examples of Belt and Road Initiative infrastructure investments include ports, skyscrapers, railroads, roads, bridges, airports, dams, coal-fired power stations, and railroad tunnels."

"Great answer!" smiles Clare, "Worthy of Mastermind!"

Grace continues, "The Chinese administration, through its Indo-Pacific strategy, intends to bolster the rule of law and human rights in regional countries facing growing influence from China. Such attention is welcome, and it has spurred numerous analyses on the drivers of China's growing influence efforts especially ones with external focus."

Christina adds, "Yes, China seeks influence due to many geo-strategic considerations, such as the protection of sea lanes critical for the transport of energy and the establishment of military facilities to protect China's growing global interests. However, much of the foundation for China's growing influence in developing countries is found inside China, where the CCP faces a mounting set of challenges to its rule that dominate its attention. It is very focused on the centralisation of power."

Grace continues her briefing, "The centralisation of power has been more an accelerant rather than the main driver of China's more assertive influence efforts. It is the Party's obsession with preserving its rule that more fundamentally drives China's growing influence in developing countries. Mounting threats to CCP control have occupied Chinese leaders as they have come to terms with the unravelling of the core factors that characterised China's reform era—relative political stability, ideological openness, and rapid economic growth."

Christina chips in, "It is different from the Russian situation. Chinese leaders have sharpened their focus on those aspects of developing country relationships likely to bolster the Party's fortunes. Two significant areas in which the CCP has stepped up influence efforts to benefit Party control are the economy and information management."

Jake frowns, "I see it differently. There isn't the same form of central governance with China, so now it wants to assert itself."

Christina nods and adds, "Yes - First, Beijing wants to mitigate mounting economic challenges and slowing growth in China through overseas investment and the creation of markets abroad for Chinese goods and materials. It's an ideal way in for China to assert itself. The Party's legitimacy depends on the health of China's economy. Access to resources needed to feed China's growing economy has long driven its engagement with the developing world, but China's economy is now struggling. Chinese leaders are looking to further boost overseas investment and trade, which have been growing for years but have been partially rebranded under the Belt and Road Initiative."

Clare looks around the room, "So what we get is China trying to copy Russia. To manipulate privatisation to such a degree that they can create a huge profit. But then to have a company which can be used for other purposes. As a laundromat for money."

Amanda speaks, "Yes, Clare, and Russia is happy to see it happen, in the knowledge that they too can leverage the situation for their own ends."

Grace adds, "And Melship and Lessiter as two hapless MPs - Only one now - used as a catalyst to generate the growth in Zillian."

"But will someone else replace Lessiter?" asks Bigsy, "Surely it can't be Andrew Brading?"

"No chance," says Clare, defensively," But I think you are on the right track. It must be someone who operates in the same circles as Melship and Lessiter."

"How about Michael Tovey?" asks Amanda, "Remember when he tried to oust Andrew Brading? He was also involved in the Elixanor situation which almost wound up with him being taken down by that hitman Yaroslev."

"He has gone to ground since then, mainly behaving as a low-key back-bencher," says Grace.

"I expect your warnings to him did some good then?" asks Bigsy.

"Or the two men that ran at him with loaded pistols. They had the larger influence," answers Amanda.

"Who are Tovey's assistants?" asks Amanda.

"I can help with that," answers Lottie, "One of them is Matt Stevens. Charming, loudmouthed, but slightly dim, actually."

Clare and Hannah both smile. They remember when Lottie had a short fling with Matt. He thought highly of himself, but inevitably crashed out under the influence of drink.

"Oh - I think I remember him too," says Jake, "He was at that Chinese in Soho. Totally out of it if I remember correctly. Oh - wasn't he your boyfriend for a while, Lottie?"

"Not something I'm too proud of," says Lottie, smiling.

"Oh yes, he was quite a loudmouth, or at least after he'd had one or two," answers Jake, "Oh, no offence Lottie"

Hannah smiles and Clare sees that Hannah knew

Matt's reputation too.

"Okay, it doesn't look as if Matt would be much help as we try to investigate Tovey."

Grace speaks, "As a matter of fact, Tovey has prior form too. He set up a trust fund in the Cayman's. The idiot gave it his own name and it all got revealed when the Panama Papers broke and exposed offshore fund hiding was big business. Of course, there were bigger fish to fry and he managed to wriggle clear of everything."

She presses another button and a list appears, illustrating some of the Panama Papers people involved.

Politicians
- Retired Member of the House of Lords
- former Member of the House of Commons
- MP and former Chief Scientific Adviser to the Ministry of Defence
- former Member of the House of Commons
- Member of the House of Lords

Relatives and associates of government officials
- Duchess and former wife of Royal.
- father of Prime Minister
- son of Baroness
- son of former Prime Minister

Businesspeople

- British political donor to the Tories and UKIP
- British retail and media moguls
- British hotelier
- British banking business executive and CEO
- former chairman of major oil company
- British-Russian oil and uranium business manager
- A Reverend and former operating officer
- British-Syrian businessman
- British entrepreneur and environmentalist
- British industrialist
- British businessman

Grace adds, "You can see from this incomplete list that there are many other higher profile people who would get 'the treatment' before Michael Tovey came to light. The list only shows part of the British involvement, altogether there are hundreds of individuals and organisations involved in dubious off-shore equity management and funds concealment."

"But what did you find out about Qiu Zhang, Grace?" asks Jake.

"Not a lot to begin with, " answers Grace, "But then I discovered that Qui Zhang was an alias. She is really known as Zhao Hu, and comes from Hong Kong, where she is linked to the (義安) Yee On triad.

"The Yee On triad is distinct from mainland Chinese criminal organisations. In ancient China, this triad was one of three major secret societies. It established branches in Macau, Hong Kong, Taiwan, and Chinese communities overseas.

"Known as 'mainland Chinese criminal organisations', they are of two major types: dark forces (loosely-organised groups) and black societies (more-mature criminal organisations).

"Two features which distinguish a black society from a dark force are the ability to achieve illegal control over local markets and receiving police protection. The Yee On triad refers to traditional criminal organisations operating in Hong Kong, Macau, Taiwan and south-east Asian countries and regions.

"We were lucky to find out anything, but four years ago, Italian police arrested 33 people connected to a Chinese triad operating in Europe as part of its Operation China Truck. The structure of the Triad placed Zhao Hu as the 'Vanguard' or Operations Master - a rank of 438, which is very close to the top. The triad were active in Tuscany, Veneto, Rome, and Milan in Italy, and in France, Spain, and Germany. The indictment accused the triad of extortion, usury, illegal gambling, prostitution, and drug trafficking. It was said to have infiltrated the transport sector, using intimidation and violence against Chinese companies wishing to transport goods by road into Europe. Police seized several vehicles, businesses, properties, and bank accounts.

Grace continues, "For this detention, it was noted

that there was a close relationship between the Triads and the Camorra, and the port of Naples is the most important landing point of the trades managed by the Chinese in cooperation with the Camorra.

Then, Grace chuckles, at what she is about to reveal, "Here's the stupidity of the system at work: Zhao Hu avoided detention, partly as a woman and because there were also two other similar ranks (both 438) which were the so-called Deputy Mountain Master and the Incense Master. A woman ranked 438 alongside two other exactly similar raked individuals. In China, you can just sense how this will play out.

"She left Hong Kong for New York the day before the arrests and there was nothing which could be done to detain her. Some say she may have shopped the triad, but there is nothing to prove it."

Grace continues, "Among the illegal activities in which the Camorra and Yee On work together are the human trafficking and illegal immigration aimed at the sexual and labour exploitation of Chinese immigrants into Italy, synthetic drug trafficking and the laundering of illicit money through the purchase of real estate.

"Then in 2017, like something from The Sopranos, investigators discovered an illicit industrial waste transportation scheme jointly run by the Camorra and Triads. The waste was transported from Italy to China, leaving from Prato in Italy and arriving in

Hong Kong - a scheme which prior to its discovery had been netting millions of dollars' worth of revenue for both organisations."

"Where there's muck there's brass," says Bigsy and Lottie laughs.

"But aren't we forgetting something?" asks Amanda, "Where that original lead that there was something off-kilter came from?"

"Oh yes, our favourite Parliamentary reporter. I've only given her very little since we returned from Gstaad. I was worried just how much could turn up in the Press," says Jake.

"Time for some disclosure, then," says Amanda, "but she must know that she cannot publish anything. Would you like me to come along?"

"That would be excellent!" says Jake, "And she will be intrigued because I think she suspects you of wiretapping her phone."

"I could not possibly comment," says Amanda.

Deflect, Distract, and Brazen it out

Jake, Clare, and Christina agreed to meet Rachel Crosby at the Cinnamon Club, a modern Indian restaurant just a short walk from Parliament.

"I was worried by the ominous words '£1 million facelift' and 'new look'," says Rachel.

"Yes, the Old Westminster Library, certainly had a refresh," says Jake.

Rachel adds, "I remember when it first launched, the Cinnamon Club became an instant London landmark. It was like an established, convivial, exclusive, old-school members' club that also happened to serve exceptionally good, high-end, modern Indian food. And women were as welcome as men. Pitch-perfect."

"I used to visit with people who thought it had been here much longer - as a restaurant, I mean," says Jake.

"I like the way the books line the main dining room as well as that gallery - most colourful," observes

Christina, "And a light touch comes from the butter-soft teal leather seating!"

"We sound like Sunday supplement restaurant critics," says Clare, "But we are here to update Rachel,"

"You know what," says Jake, "This food is so good, I think we should order one starter and one main each and then share!"

There was a pause as they considered and Jake made a list, ready for the waiter.

"If only Bigsy, with his appetite was here!" says Clare, "We wouldn't have to worry about the quantity," They all laugh.

Rachel suggests they all try the Twisted Tea, combining Tanqueray No10 gin, saffron-steeped Galliano and both chamomile liquor and tea.

"This is going to be one of those evenings," says Jake, as the small wagon arrived with the drinks.

They start to recount their story of the trip to Geneva, and then onward to Gstaad. Rachel was most interested, but when they mentioned the names of the people they had met in Gstaad, she stopped them.

"My brother David knew Miller McDonald and Qiu Zhang," she says. "He met them both in London a couple of times. It was something to do with UK

Government business. He explained it to me once, but it seemed to me to be secret-squirrel type surveillance."

"I can't properly understand why he would be talking to those two about UK Government business?" says Clare.

"To be truthful, neither can I," answers Rachel, "I think he was trying to set up a combined deal with Brant Industries. Using his computer technology and their existing 'ins' to the UK Government. If it had worked, they would have had a compelling proposition, although I'm not sure most MPs would like the idea of being monitored."

"What happened?" asks Jake.

They all paused the conversation as a couple of waiters appeared. The waiters set up a small table next to their own and then carefully place an array of starters upon it. The lead waiter then produces four small plates which he ceremoniously distributes around the table. Then, in turn, each of the starters was brought forward.

"Here we are," he explains, "Spiced aubergine steak, pumpkin chutney, masala peanut and moutabal; Tandoori octopus with chutney potatoes and tomato lemon dressing; Char-grilled Zeeland kingfish with carom seed, samphire and pickled radish and Lamb mille-feuille – Hyderabadi black spiced lamb escalope, Awadhi lamb galouti!"

"Amazing!" says Clare, "I can't think why I've never been here before!"

Rachel continues with her story, "Well the whole deal with Brant collapsed when David died. The only record of it was on his laptop, and although I still have it, it has proved impossible to get into with his passwords and other security measures. Remember, he was in the business!"

"I know this is delicate," says Jake, "So please excuse me for asking, but do you suspect foul play for your brother's death?"

The normally professional Rachel looks a little tearful, "Yes, I do, actually. David was too positive in his outlook to have driven all the way to Liverpool and then killed himself in a dockyard pool."

Christina nods, "I assume the police were involved in full investigation?"

Rachel nods, "Yes, they were, and said they would leave no stone unturned, although I was not convinced. The un-investigated laptop is a case in point. The same with his forensically clean car, found parked near to the scene. That short log file I was sent by email from him. None of it makes sense. I think I said the police left it as an open verdict."

Jake answers, "We could get our technical whizz on to this. To look at the log file and to see if it is possible to break into David's computer."

Clare realises that Jake was suggesting Bigsy could take a look.

"You are most welcome, but please remember that this was all looked at by the police at the time," replies Rachel.

"Where is the computer now?" asks Christina.

"It's in my apartment," says Rachel, "In the bottom of my wardrobe, actually."

"Okay, we'll send someone around tomorrow to pick it up."

"The same rules still apply to all of this," says Clare "Just to be clear, we can't have any of this in the press - at least not at the moment,"

"We are long past that moment," says Rachel, "Rest assured that we are good. I'm treating this as a personal situation rather than part of my investigative journalism."

"Okay, so that's what we need to pick your brains about next, Rachel. I'm hoping you'll be outspoken because this is simply between the four of us. We'd like to know what your opinion is of Michael Tovey, MP?"

Rachel grimaces, "Tovey? A snake, I'd say. A privileged Etonian with no moral compass."

"Oh, we've hit a nerve?" asks Clare.

"I'm afraid that Tovey's behaviour and attitudes are typical of some parts of the British establishment. If the ruling party has a shared culture, it's entitlement and shamelessness, a conviction that wrongdoing should meet consequences only if you are poor and powerless."

"He sounds like a few others I could mention!" interjects Jake.

"When Tovey joined the old leadership during the pandemic, he made it very clear that he believed that the rules had to accommodate his needs, rather than vice versa,"

"I remember - he was one of the people caught partying during the lockdowns," says Clare.

Rachel adds, "He was the same with the multitude of expenses scandals: he was one of the MPs who railed against 'benefit cheats' while milking hard-pressed taxpayers. His immediate circle of friends believed they were not sufficiently remunerated and that offshore tax havens were the way to go. All the time he was cultivating party donors – the City hotshots and top lawyers with whom he clinked champagne glasses. "

"The penalties were so light for most of them," said Clare.

Rachel continues, "Why shouldn't they just help

themselves to extras they deserved? A handful of MPs went to prison, but for most, being personally winded by some adverse newspaper headlines did not prove a roadblock to their future political careers. In a few cases they even made political capital because it raised their profile."

Jake considered, "The revolving door between the fourth estate and politics has enjoyed a bit-part in this scandal. Remember the press officer/woman journalist who ended up being thrown under the ex-PM's bus (metaphorically) to keep some others in power. Still, I suppose she owned up, which is more than can be said for most of the inner circle."

Rachel nodded, "Yes - Tovey discovered that spreading myths and outright lies about benefit claimants, refugees and Muslims was largely consequence-free. Tovey is one of the MPs who emphasises the establishment's unofficial motto: 'rules for thee and not for me.' He is adept at firing chaff like some lumbering warplane to deflect any arguments, whether against him or in defence of his party leaders. One of the Pomps – pompous – oh - I'll let you guess what the 'S' stands for."

"I like the imagery of the warplane with sparks flying out from it to confuse incoming missiles," chuckled Jake.

Rachel continues, "Tovey boasted that nobody 'stuck up for the bankers as much as I did' after the last financial crash. Indeed, Tovey has been a longstanding and unapologetic champion of the wealthiest, who he once described as a 'put-upon minority' who made a 'heroic contribution'. They barely needed his defence."

"I assume he was richly rewarded for running to their defence?" asks Jake.

Their table had been cleared and now the main course arrived. Jake noticed that the waiters had assembled two small serving tables for this.

"I think we may have over-ordered!" he said, smiling.

The waiter patiently explains the new dishes: "Now the main courses: Achari gobhi - Tandoori cauliflower with pickling spices, yoghurt sauce, pilau rice; Kokum crusted halibut on the bone, shallot and tamarind sauce, lemon rice; Grilled New Caledonian Obsiblue king prawns, Alleppey curry sauce, rice vermicelli; Vesavara spiced free range chicken breast, chicken leg stew, stir-fried greens. And, of course, the accompaniments: Tandoori breads; Potato paratha, garlic & coriander naan, tandoori whole wheat roti; Homemade chutneys; Pilau and lemon rice."

Clare comments again, "It all looks amazing!"

Rachel continues her story, "Then, to Jake's point, after the financial crisis, over 300 financiers were convicted of crimes after the financial system nearly collapsed in the US. Here in the UK, the number of bankers who went to prison was just five. Five!

Again: terrible behaviour, minimal consequences. Aided and abetted by the softly spoken words from Tovey."

She adds, "There are good reasons why members of the establishment like Tovey may believe their power and connections are a bullet-proof vest. "

"But I thought Tovey had been hunted any gunmen and rescued by Amanda Millers' people?" asks Jake.

Rachel nods, "Yes, if the rumours are true, but I think the source of those incoming gangsters was more connected with his other shady dealings."

Then she pauses before saying, "I know I can't publish this but consider that in the UK, you are over 20 times more likely to be prosecuted for benefit fraud than tax fraud. Benefit fraud may inflict far less economic and social harm, but our society hysterically demands that it's the sins of the poor that must be punished. Oh yes, Tovey is an arch exponent of 'deflect, distract and brazen it out.' "

Committee Room

Clare was back in Parliament with Lottie and Hannah. They were sitting in a deserted meeting room on a quiet Friday afternoon. Conventionally Fridays were quiet in Parliament. Like a public school, sitting was scheduled only from 9.30am to 3pm and no debates were scheduled for Fridays, so many MPs did not even bother to stay around the buildings.

It meant that there were usually free rooms around the Estate and Lottie had co-opted one, via the W4MP website. They were in a Committee Room and the electronic diary indicated that it would next be used for a Formal Meeting of the Health and Social Care Committee on the following Monday afternoon.

Lottie, Hannah, Clare, Bigsy, Christina and Jake were all present and they had the session listed by Lottie as the 'Transport Technical Committee debrief of Working Papers.'

"I wanted to make it sound boring, so we don't attract any attention," explained Lottie.

"Doesn't sound boring to me!" chipped in Bigsy.

"Bigsy, you are sometimes special," commented Clare.

The room's capacity was much larger than the assembled group and a set of ancient wooden tables and chairs had been pulled into a 'U' shape which took up much of the room. The carpeting was like something from a 1970's pub, and the wallpaper above the panelling on the walls was a swirly salmon colour. A TV annunciator on one wall was soundlessly playing back the empty chamber from the House of Commons.

"I drove over to Rachel's and brought back her brother's PC," explained Bigsy, "I took a quick look, but have given it to someone else with some specialist knowledge to 'spring the catches' on it. Then we'll be able to look for anything interesting. I also got the file that had been sent to Rachel. It looks like a tiny file from a PC almost like a serial number or something, so I don't think I'll have any trouble decoding it, especially when we have the PC 'opened,'

"But can you trust your friend?" asked Lottie, "I mean, he won't start publicising what we are doing or anything like that?"

"No, Luke is a good guy - a friend with whom I have

been involved in numerous scrapes over the year. I trust him implicitly - as does he, towards me."

"When do you think it will be ready?" asked Clare, "I mean that we can access it?"

"Knowing Luke, it will be ready this evening. I'll have to collect it from him."

"What else do we know?" asked Clare, "Or at least suspect?"

"It looks to me as if Michael Tovey might be taking the place of Douglas Lessiter in the Zillian scheme," said Lottie, "I was in the office yesterday and who should walk in? None other than Tovey. Embarrassingly he had Matt Stevens with him. But Tovey and Melship were making jokes and it was clear that they are old drinking buddies. It seems they go back a long way."

"Right the way back to Oxford, by the look of it," said Jake who was looking at his laptop, "They were both members of the same drinking club, where they had to meet in a pub, carrying a diamond and a toy squirrel and order a pint of Champagne."

"Boy's toys," said Clare, and Christina agreed.

"It all makes sense of the big parties that Melship had, too. Cultivating his chumocracy," said Lottie, "I used to go to them in the early days, but then I felt I'd heard every chat-up line ever invented and decided to stop going. I know, I still ended up with

Matt, but that's another story."

"Hmm. I seem to remember a few others too," said Hannah, smiling, "Both before and after Matt..."

"Okay, point taken!" said Lottie, "But how's this relevant?"

"Only in much as if you can remember any of them, for their backgrounds?" asked Christina.

"Oh yes, they were mainly well-heeled, well turned out, polite," answered Lottie, "But they all had serious defects,"

"Ooh, interesting..." Said Clare, "Like what?"

Lottie opened up, "Well, Davy was a serial buffoon, like a clown act. All the time. He thought it endearing. Matt was a loudmouth who couldn't hold his drink and was totally indiscreet. Brian (yes that was really his name) was charming but ran out of interesting things to say after about three sentences. Denzil was funny but had a chip on his shoulder. Not the obvious one, but one about how his family had treated him badly. I could go on, but you get the picture, without me even going upstairs."

"Going upstairs; That's a great euphemism," said Jake.

"Oh, we used it all the time around at the flat," said Clare.

"And elsewhere," added Hannah.

Clare summarised, "Okay, so Tovey has replaced Lessiter in the scam, which requires the combined - er - talents of Melship and Tovey. At the end of it, they both stand to make decent off-shore money."

"Yes, that's the sum of it," said Jake, "We could take it back to Amanda, but I think she's already reached that conclusion."

Recording

Bigsy was in the Triangle offices. His friend Luke had returned David Crosby's computer. Sure enough, Luke had defeated the laptop's security and been able to access the hard drive. Bigsy had made a copy of the hard drive and was pouring through the emails.

"Nothing unusual," he said out loud, when a ping arrived on his text.

It was from Luke and said, "Not sure whether you noticed the second partition?"

Bigsy hadn't. He had made a simple copy of the disk to work upon, but somehow didn't spot that the disk had been divided into two sections. A readily accessible one and another, smaller hidden section.

"Luke - Thank you!" he sent and proceeded to copy the second section to another hard drive, so that he was sure to preserve the original.

"Encryption Key Required:" said his copy routine. He typed in a string of characters and noticed that a dash was being inserted by the system after every fourth keystroke. He needed a 20 character-long key to allow the disk to be read and copied back in an un-encoded state.

He remembered the key that had been sent to Rachel in the mystery email. It was the right length. He typed it in.

'AHfg-1265-WeUI-7602-QmaL'

"Encryption Key Accepted:" said the copy routine. He watched as a giant copy operation began. In around half an hour he would have the contents of the secret folder stored on David Crosby's computer.

PART THREE

lived in bars

We've lived in bars
And danced on the tables
Hotels, trains and ships that sail
We swim with sharks
And fly with aeroplanes in the air

We know your house so very well
And we will wake you once we've walked up all your stairs

There's nothing like living in a bottle
And nothing like ending it all for the world
We're so glad you have come back
Every living lion will lay in your lap

We know your house so very well
And we will bust down your door if you're not there

We've lived in bars
And danced on tables
Hotels, trains and ships that sail
We swim with sharks
And fly with aeroplanes out of here

Charlyn (Chan) Marie Marshall

Partition revealed

Bigsy waited and could see the file structure emerging on the new disk. Much of it was references to other companies, but then he noticed Zillian appear. He should be able to start from there.

Once completed, he dug into the Zillian folder. There were several documents, mercifully without any additional passwords.

He selected the one that said 'IPO of Zillian' which included a Process folder.

There was a form S-1 registration statement; the list of SEC technical requirements; A Registration Statement filing, then the S-1 Filing and the complete execution timeline mapped out. The whole Zillian flotation was poised and ready to roll.

Bigsy noticed the Tactics folder. It included several small recordings in it as well as a couple of documents.

He clicked the first recording.

"Hi, this is David Crosby, I'm in trouble related to the Zillian launch and am putting my statement on record. It is also saved away to a DropBox folder in the Cloud, so even if the original data here on my PC is compromised, it should still be available from the DropBox backup."

Bigsy knew that using DropBox for a backup was a rudimentary solution, but could understand why Crosby, in an emergency, had done it.

Crosby's voice continued, "I've discovered some big irregularities with the Zillian launch. The documents in this folder prove the accusations I am making on this recording."

"Firstly, Zillian doesn't have any vehicles of its own. The ones it is selling are from a Chinese factory making clones of other vehicles.

"Secondly, the electric cars are a sham. Zillian is buying chassis from another well-known German car manufacturer and adding their own bodies to them. They only need a few to prove the point for their share valuation.

"Thirdly, the contracts being entered into by Zillian, for example, with the UK Government are being made under a mixture of threats and bribery. Threats because they had compromised information about some key MPs and bribery because they are also providing the same MPs with cash to invest in the new company.

"I don't know who orchestrated this, but I suspect the Chinese are putting up most of the capital for the equity launch. With good management, the shares should rise considerably.

"Then, I believe there will be some kind of 'good news' press release which will add even more to the share prices. My suspicion is that this will be because the UK Government wants build good relationships and an order book with Zillian."

The recording stopped. Bigsy considered for a moment. It seemed as if David had been prepared to whistle blow this whole situation. Instead, he had paid with his life.

Bigsy realised this was dangerous knowledge. He would move the laptop to his off-site store where he kept the disaster recovery used by The Triangle. It was in a vault in north-east London.

Bigsy emailed the recording to himself, carefully changing its filetype to that of a spreadsheet first, to make it harder to track. Now was time to convene a meeting with everyone.

What we've found

Bigsy arranged to meet everyone in the Triangle's own offices on Thamesside, in their office building in Hays Galleria. Everyone knew the location and he considered it to be even more secure from wiretaps than the Parliamentary Estate.

He invited Amanda Miller and Grace Fielding to join remotely, as well as Hannah, Lottie plus the usual gang of Christina, Clare, and Jake. Amanda would patch Grace in from GCHQ. Because of the sensitive nature of the meeting, he decided not to invite Rachel Crosby.

Bigsy described the situation to everyone, including a playback of the recording from Rachel's brother David. Jake named the two MPs now suspected of involvement in the scheme to float Zillian and to make a huge profit for themselves.

"I can't deny that this is well-researched," said Amanda, "But the burden of proof still runs against us. Ever since that smoking gun when a one-time

Prime Minister attempted to lie his way out of a situation. Remember even when 300 photographs appeared, he was still saying he'd broken no rules, and that he didn't know anything about it. It was like an upgrade of 'plausible deniability', through "I cannot recollect" and onwards to bare-faced denials."

"What are you saying, then?" asked Christina, "It sounds as if we need to catch them in the act of their scam?"

"I'm afraid so, and there are several moving parts. However, if we catch them and can prove that we have evidence, then I think events would take their own course. Neither the Chinese nor the Russians like failure, nor being found out!"

"Well, we have good access," said Christina, "I mean Lottie has a direct line to Melship and we also have a link to one of Tovey's assistants."

"We do, although that is less helpful, because he is an unreliable blabbermouth," said Jake, speaking up on Lottie's behalf.

"That's right, but I think his weakness could become our strength," said Lottie, "Matt Stevens always likes to hear good gossip and likes to think he hears it first. What could be better than an old 'ex' of his asking him for some advice, ideally over copious amounts of alcohol."

"Will he still meet you?" asked Hannah, "You know

how you left it?"

"Oh yes, I think so, time will have played its part and I think he'd have a certain dry pleasure in seeing me asking his opinion of something. It will need to be work-related though..."

"What about something to do with the car industry? You must be so well briefed by now?" suggested Jake.

"I know, something about electric cars and their chargers being prepared for widespread distribution in London?" suggested Bigsy, "But that London is to be made even more car-free?"

"That could work." said Grace, "Especially if part of the share price launch is predicated on doing a big deal with London."

"It would ruin the IPO share launch of Zillian, which would not make the big money after all."

"So why are you asking Matt about this?" asked Christina, "There has to be a very plausible reason?"

"You can say you want to know whether to stop Melship from making a fool of himself, not with the share deal, of which you can be ignorant, but because you think Melship is about to advise the PM to make some kind of stirring speech in Parliament, which would all be wrong a few days later and lead to a massive U-turn."

"I like it," said Jake.

"Oh yes, that could very well create a meltdown and see the way open for Opposition attack," said Grace, "Back-bench Tories are looking for an opportunity to move the PM, to get someone more likeable before the next election."

Amanda spoke, "Conservative governments in the past have regularly suffered humiliating meltdowns. In 1990 Margaret Thatcher's premiership ended in tears after months of plotting against her. Then her successor, John Major, resigned as leader and sought re-election in a failed attempt to silence his critics."

"Oh yes, we forget that it has always been so," acknowledged Jake.

Amanda continued, "More recently, the crises have come faster and faster: David Cameron's resignation after losing his Brexit referendum in 2016; Theresa May's disastrous attempt to increase her parliamentary majority in 2017; the failed effort to remove her through a no-confidence vote in 2018; her repeated Brexit defeats before her resignation in 2019."

"Yes, they seem to speed up in more recent times, " added Clare

Amanda added, "Curiously, none of these episodes led to the Conservatives losing office. On each occasion, for days, weeks or months, the party's future appeared to hang in the balance. We've all seen the journalists reporting excitedly from Downing Street, or outside meetings of the Tories' much-mythologised 1922 Committee. Opposition parties seized on Conservative divisions and disarray. Labour politicians began to believe they might soon take office."

Now Clare spoke, "Every time, the sense of crisis gradually ebbed away. The Conservatives changed their leader, or some of their policies, or just played for time, exploiting the opportunities in Britain's parliamentary calendar for evasion and delay. With its frequent recesses, the House of Commons is not as tough a place for wounded prime ministers as is traditionally claimed."

Amanda looked serious, "I have to remain impartial in this because of my role, but it's easy to note that Tory governments survive their disastrous phases partly because voters lose interest. Not just because most people only follow politics closely for, at best, a few days at a time. But also, because these very social media compatible crises can be emotionally and politically satisfying in themselves - like some tawdry soap-opera."

Lottie smiled, "This could be a great story for Matt. The potential overthrow of the Conservatives because of his own Minister's avoidable mistake. I like it!"

Breaking up with a drunkard

Lottie was about to meet Matt Stevens. She had not seen him since their break-up, which she had engineered to be on a commuter train, early evening, before he had a chance to get drunk.

It hadn't gone especially well, although it had created a fascinating spectacle for those sitting in the adjacent seats. Lottie had also enlisted Tessa's support and she had sat across the gangway from Matt and Lottie when the event occurred.

Of course, in the style of the best breakups it was all done in a very public place, to avoid the worst of Matt's protestations. Lottie decided that Matt must have had a liquid lunch, in any case, because he didn't have too much logic in his replies, and the whole scene was over between Vauxhall and Putney, where Lottie and Tessa left the train.

Lottie had called Matt plaintively this time:

"Matt? Its Lottie...I hope we are still able to talk.

Look I've found out something. It's about your boss, Michael Tovey. I think you need to know and maybe give me advice about what I should do with what I've found out."

"Lottie?! I didn't expect to hear from you again! This is quite a surprise! How are you doing? Erm, you know I'm with Charlotte Mendez now? That's Charlotte from Banca Cariba. She doesn't work on the Estate. But sure, if you think I can help, then fire away!"

"I'm doing fine, by the way. This topic is rather sensitive, I'll need to meet you for half an hour somewhere close to Parly. Do you know Cafe Churchill on Parliament Street?"

"What the place near to Downing Street? Near the traffic lights?"

"That's the one. Can we meet there for breakfast, say tomorrow? At 8.30?"

"Sure, I'll be along. Mine's a latte and a croissant!"

Lottie had picked a low-key place to meet, one that most resembled a work venue.

Cafe Churchill

The next morning, Lottie was early to arrive at the Cafe. There were a few tables with chequered tablecloth along the pavement and a couple of other consultant/refugees from Parliament sitting hunched over another table, engrossed in a pre-bid discussion.

Then she saw Matt arrive. He was walking briskly and looked fresher than Lottie could ever remember. Maybe this Charlotte was having a good effect upon him.

But then, as he approached the table, she sensed the aroma of peppermint, aftershave, and stale beer. At least he had made some attempt to disguise it, but she realised that this was the same old Matt, still spending his evenings in bars.

"Hello, my darling," he said, and Lottie remembered that Matt was originally from Cornwall and that 'Darling' was part of his workaday vocabulary, just like 'My beauty'.

"I was inside and ordered your latte and a croissant," answered Lottie, "I haven't got long to explain this to you,"

"Okay, it sounds like some juicy gossip, especially if it has to be delivered in person," said Matt.

The coffees and croissants arrived and they both paused to take a bite and to realise that the lattes were too hot to drink.

"Okay, here's the situation," said Lottie. "You know I am working for Duncan Melship? Well, I recently went on a trip with him and Duggie Lessiter to Switzerland."

"Oh wow, you are moving up in the world!" said Matt.

"Well, Melship is now involved with the car industry, and I think Michael Tovey has now taken over from Lessiter, since Lessiter's tragic accident."

"Yes, it was tragic. First Isabella and then Duggie."

"Yes, well my friend Hannah also worked for Douglas Lessiter, and we heard some of the inside story. We heard that electric cars and their chargers are being prepared for widespread distribution in London? - It's some big propaganda push announced by the PM, driven by Michael Tovey's agenda and briefings."

"Yes, it's almost good to go. It will make quite a lavish splash," said Matt,"I know it is technically insider trading, but there's a few companies who will see share prices rise on the back of this story. In fact, I have heard Tovey talk about a particular company - Zillian - which he thinks could go through the roof."

"Well, I'm not so worried about share prices, " lied Lottie, "But I am interested in stopping the PM from making an absolute fool of himself in Parliament."

"How so?"

"Well, there are strong rumours that London is to be made even more car-free," explained Lottie "It would seem crazy to roll out a massive infrastructure to one part of the country that didn't need it. The red wall towns in the north could have a field day - 'Wasting money on London when the rest of the country is crying out for new infrastructure.' "

Lottie could now sip from the latte. She paused to look at Matt's expression. Was he taking it all in?

She continued, "I can see that there is something very 'profile enhancing' for someone to stop the whole process before it goes too far. It would save the PM from getting more egg on his face at a time when his support is somewhat beleaguered."

"I can see that. How reliable are your sources?"

"It's not so much about the sources, as about the ability to put the big picture together. Look in yesterday's Metro, you'll see the story about how London plans to reduce the number of cars still further. Look, I brought the article."

Lottie fished in her bag and brought out a press cutting from yesterday's paper.

"Wowowow. Okay, Lottie, so what do you want?" asked Matt.

"Matt, I don't want anything. I'm just concerned that your Minister doesn't make a huge mistake that could bring the whole government crashing down. I guess you, rather than me will be the hero of the piece, but I'll bank that for another time," Lottie smiled, sipped the last from her latte and then stood.

"I need to go now, Matt," she said as Matt hastily stood and then made a motion as if to shake her hand.

"So formal, Matt, but I shall now leave this in your capable hands," she turned and rapidly walked back along Parliament Street in the direction of the Houses of Parliament. Matt was still clutching the press cutting as he stood and then scurried away towards The Treasury buildings in Whitehall.

"That went well," said one of the two consultants sitting at the adjacent table. Bigsy nodded back at Jake, "Yes and I think we should have a good video of the entire encounter."

Clare's article

Rachel Crosby's phone rang.

"Hi Rachel, it's Clare. We've found something out about your brother now and we want to share it with you."

"What? Have you found something on his laptop?"

"Oh yes, it's in his own words too, a recording that show he was into the situation quite deep."

"Oh, okay, I knew it, does it shed any light on his death?"

"It adds to the evidence that he was murdered," said Clare, "And Rachel, I've written an article which it would be good to get into the papers under your by-line. It is a prediction of some stormy water ahead for the current Prime Minister."

"Won't that be yesterday's news?" asked Rachel, "I mean he is only just clinging on as it is!"

"This might just be enough to tip it over the edge when some other news breaks," answered Clare, "It should be in your in-box."

Rachel read Clare's article:

"By exposing the errors and shortcomings of our usual ruling class, and by forcing them into U-turns, changes of leadership and displays of sometimes embarrassing contrition, Conservative crises can feel like a rebalancing between politicians and citizens — and make more fundamental change seem unnecessary.

"The 1992 and 2019 elections both came after particularly protracted periods of Tory upheaval. Yet they saw the biggest total Conservative votes of the past half-century.

"Many people seemed to feel that the Tories had listened and adapted sufficiently to their discontents. The government had been punished enough, so ironically a new one was not needed.

"In pre-democratic times, the status quo was protected by brief, pressure-releasing ruptures in the established order. In medieval France, for example, the annual Feast of Fools would be when low-ranking clergy temporarily swapped places with their superiors and mockery of church practices was permitted.

"There is something similarly ritualised in today's Tory crises: from the theatrical sending of letters to the 1922 Committee by MPs seeking a leadership contest, to the inauthentic-feeling attacks on the government by the right-wing press, which flare up and then suddenly cease.

"These protagonists may well be playing their roles on the understanding that uncomfortable periods for the Tories are the necessary price, paid every few years, for the party's long-term dominance. And during these crises British politics becomes, more than ever, mostly about the Conservatives.

"They know how to do theatricality and how to cling to Power.

"For non-Tories, trying to work out who would be the least awful new Tory leader is a familiar routine — in effect, a partial acceptance of continuing Conservative rule.

"Many voters and journalists probably know more about the rules of Tory leadership contests than they do about Labour's policies. And that's not just because they don't have enough compelling ones. There is an English preoccupation with Tory politics that is a kind of self-fulfilling prophecy.

"In one-party states, it's common to ridicule or feel contempt for your government without being able to envisage its removal.

"Our politics isn't that stuck, yet, despite the Tories' ongoing efforts to tilt the electoral system in their favour, such as making it harder to vote for social groups who tend not to support them or gerrymandering political boundaries.

"But the deepening cynicism about politicians means that a chaotic government no longer shocks and alienates voters as much as it did in previous eras with struggling prime ministers were ejected from Downing Street for smaller errors than those of the current gangster-like incumbent.

"Nowadays it's widely expected that our leaders will be out of their depth, as well as entirely out for themselves.

"Yet it's too early to be sure that the Tories' current troubles will recede in the usual way. There is another, rarer kind of Conservative crisis. It is less exciting to follow, but longer lasting and more lethal. It involves enough voters firmly deciding that the Tories have been in power for too long, and then fitting every government scandal and mistake into that template.

"The last time this happened was in the 1990s, when Labour's return to office was preceded by almost five years of Tory calamities and failed relaunches. Tony Blair was Labour leader for the most decisive part of the period, and his ability to promise a better future helped make the Conservative government look obsolete.

"Current Labour doesn't have the same salesman's gifts. Nor does it get much of a hearing from wavering Tory voters and the right-wing press.

"We live in a more tribal age.

"It's also a more impatient one, jittered by social media when the political mood quickly changes. The Tories could be in the early stages of a terminal crisis. But if you're hoping that they really are doomed this time, it's going to be an anxious wait."

"Wow, Clare" said Rachel, "That's not bad, I can tell you have written PR for corporates! - I might need to ease the tone a little for a leader article, but it is quite do-able."

"And the consequences?" asked Clare.

"Quite acceptable, we have for a long time tried to course-correct the government, so this won't seem out of place."

Floundering

Things were chaotic in Michael Tovey's office at Parliament. Here was a man tipped for the very top, but now floundering around about what to say and whether to warn the Prime Minister of what he had just heard from Matt Stevens.

"Matt, you are absolutely sure about this?" he asked again, "I mean, so far I have remained loyal to the Prime Minister during the scandals. I even called him an 'exceptional leader' who is 'good at thinking things others aren't thinking' - but let's face it, he is no Churchill.

"Churchill always had new ideas. The PM may eschew conventional thought, but his increasing desperation is driven by his own self-interest, and forgetfully he will change positions between interviews to suit the cameras."

He added: "I'm just saying that the politicians who succeed are the ones with a willingness to make decisions and to then persuade people. I think it might be time for us to up the ante."

"What are you suggesting?" asked Matt, somewhat confused.

"I'm just considering letting the PM announce the cars and chargers plan for London. It could be my chance for a crack at the main job."

Matt asked, "But won't the London initiative blow up in his face? Apart from the lower car targets for London, there's the whole Levelling Up of the north. It would look doubly stupid to announce a major investment plan for London when the north is crying out for infrastructure. And it could easily annoy the London Mayor too!"

"Yes, but that is the beauty of our Prime Minister. His crowded brain is overflowing with scandals, and the web of lies that he spins. He is also without any bright tacticians in his office now, just 'yes men and women' prepared to take the money whilst secretly loathing the way he is running things."

"Matt, can you run that advancement of the London Infrastructure up into a speech, which the PM could give in the House. Notice how I am trusting you with something big here."

Matt nodded, pleased at the privileged position that he had attained, but worried that this was not the plan he had envisaged after the coffee with Lottie.

Safe to cross streets

An hour after Matt's exchange with Michael Tovey, an incoming phone call to Tovey's office was answered by Matt.

"Hello, this is Miller McDonald, from Brant. I need to speak urgently to Michael Tovey. He will know the topic."

Matt relayed the information and ten minutes later Tovey was on his way to a meeting with McDonald. Matt noticed that Tovey didn't use a pool car, but instead ordered a regular London Taxi.

Tovey arrived at the nearby St Ermin's hotel in St James a few minutes later and was shown to a room, set up for a conference. There were several people in the room. He recognised Miller McDonald, and thought he recognised another woman, but had no idea about the others, all in suits but looking just a little like they were back from a battle-zone. Before he had a chance to run introductions, another door opened and in walked Duncan Melship, also unaccompanied.

"Oh, hello Duncan, I hadn't expected you to be here."

"Gentlemen, gentlemen, and ladies, of course," said Miller McDonald. He looked across to Melship and Tovey, "It is a great honour to have two of UK's Members of Parliament present, and even more so that they followed instructions to come alone.

"Let me introduce the rest of us here today, "Miller McDonald and Mary Ranzino from Brant and Qiu Zhang and Kirillka Valeryevich representing Zillian."

"Let me come straight to the point," said Miller.

He continued, "We have been preparing this New York Stock Exchange launch of Zillian for some time now, and it is ready for next week. We have also been preparing a few press releases to assist its price go up upon launch. Both of our dear colleagues, the two MPs, have an important part to play for that reason.

"Firstly, Douglas Melship, Secretary of State for Department for Transport Efficiency- DfTE must meet his obligation to place a significant order for the UK, with Zillian. Some 10,000 government service vehicles will be provided on a rental agreement from Zillian.

"Then, Michael Tovey, will provide the Prime Minister with the House of Commons announcement to provide framework legislation to support vital changes to the UK's infrastructure, starting with London.

"But that could ruin the Prime Minister," said Tovey, "London is trying to drastically reduce the number of cars."

McDonald continued, "It doesn't matter. The Prime Minister is well-known as a serial liar. If he says one thing today and does something completely different tomorrow no-one - and I mean no-one - will be surprised."

"But he could lose his job over this. Too much accumulated reputational damage?" said Melship.

McDonald again, "But think of the upside. You both get rich on next week's share price lift and then you also get a crack at the top jobs in Parliament following a leadership contest."

Melship asked, "But what about the company? Zillian. It can't actually manufacture the vehicles, can it?"

McDonald answered, "No, but how long will it take before that is discovered? Plenty of time to divest and cash in big time. And China gets a ready-made laundry mechanism for cleaning cashflow. Converting cloned inexpensive vehicles into cleaned money."

"Not to mention the vast requirement for

component parts," added the Mary Ranzino, "They can be cleared through the same laundering process."

"You learn well," said Valeryevich, "It is an approach we have used in Mother Russia since after the fall of the USSR."

"This has become bigger than I expected," said Melship.

"Well, you can soon enjoy your good fortune. And you need to know you are safe crossing those busy London streets," said Valeryevich.

The threat was not wasted on Tovey nor Melship.

Badge engineering

Christina was in The Triangle offices with Jake, Clare and Bigsy.

"There's still something about all of this situation that doesn't quite ring true," she said.

"How so?" asked Bigsy, "I mean, we've found the two shaky MPs about to pull a stunt to raise Zillian's share price and walk away with a tidy profit."

"I know," said Christina, "That's the obvious situation. I think there must be something more."

"Okay," said Clare, "Let's think about it...A car company launched on the American stock market, but only making its cars in China. Owned mainly by Chinese."

"But with indirect links to Russia," added Christina, "But not to the Kremlin, instead to a bratva gang."

"And making its cars look as if they are British,

European and American," added Jake, "Like, say Ford or BMW,"

"It means they will have a lot of cars in transit," said Bigsy, "You know, ships filled with them,"

"So, they will bring these cars halfway round the world to sell into local European markets?" asked Clare.

Jake said, "Before they invest in local factories, like Nissan still do, from Sunderland and Honda did, from Swindon - until mid 2021. I expect they will wait until there's some form of deal available."

Clare added, "Yes, but Honda closed the factory and turned it over to a logistics developer. The developer makes tin-shed depots and then leases them out to mega-online retailers. Companies like Amazon."

Jake said, "Yes, and Honda will make its new cars in Japan, to ship to Europe. It was fall-out from Brexit. The EU cut a new deal with Japan."

Clare agreed, looking at her laptop, "It is interesting to notice that Zillian wants to copy some of this process. They already make cars in Guangzhou, China, for example. Honda Accord, Honda City, Honda Crider, Honda Crosstour, Honda Fit, Honda Odyssey and Honda Vezel,"

Bigsy said, "I've never heard of some of those makes. Are you sure they are not motorcycles?"

Clare answered, "No, I'm certain they are all types of cars. Look - here's some pictures from the Honda website."

"So have we got any closer to working this out?" asked Christina, "There has to be an angle on it."

Jake ventured, "Something to do with the importation of cars? Re-branding them to look British? Remember when General Motors used to call their cars Vauxhall in the UK and Opel in Europe? It implied they were made in Germany."

Bigsy added, "And come to think of it, they were Holden in Australia and Buick, Saturn, and Cadillac in the USA. Badge engineering, they call it."

Clare added, "And since 2021 they are owned by that well-known brand Stellantis!"

"Stellantis?" queried Bigsy, "Never heard of them!"

Clare added, still looking at her laptop, "Stellantis is the sixth-largest automaker worldwide, they design, develop, manufacture and sell automobiles bearing the brands of Abarth, Alfa Romeo, Chrysler, Citroën, Dodge, DS, Fiat, Jeep, Lancia, Maserati, Opel, Peugeot, Ram and Vauxhall, and Mopar auto parts!"

"Okay, so now we are on to something," said Christina, "Zillian joins the ranks of shadowy companies owning big brands and shipping their products quietly around the world."

"I can think of some other organisations that would like to be able to stealthily move product around," said Clare.

"Exactly," said Christina.

"And I think I need someone else to help us now," said Clare, "It's another flatmate, or at least it would have been if I still lived in Bermondsey!"

Advice

Clare called in on her old flat. Tessa was beside herself with excitement and had clearly been told of recent adventures by Lottie. Clare wondered how much Katharina Maier - Cat- would know about what was happening.

"Hey everyone, I think I'm going to need some help!" said Clare, opening a cool bag containing three bottles of chilled wine.

"That wine should help us all think," said Lottie.

"I want to know about an IPO, " explained Clare, "The one for the car company, Zillian."

Cat smiled; Clare realised that she must know most of what had happened.

"Oh no, I swear I haven't told anyone else," said Cat, "But it is a great story."

"I had a look at Zillian's offering as well. It reads as

if the figures have been highly manipulated, like they are really trying to make this seem good. Almost too good."

Clare asked, "So, will traders buy it?"

"I'd say it is a slender share. It is one of those which looks too good to be true, which could put a lot of people off. I can see you might get some high-volume trades at the start of the day, but they will all have disinvested by the end of the day."

"But what about if the company received some good news?" asked Clare.

Cat answered, "Ew, that could be illegal. It could smack of insider trading. The company would have the SEC down on them."

Cat continued, "It's being launched next week, isn't it? On the New York Stock Exchange? I guess they are hoping it will be a rocket ship like some of the other car companies."

"Can you take the day off? I mean when it launches, to be in our office and to give us some guidance?" asked Clare.

"What? A chance to be in on one of Lottie's friend's schemes? How could I turn it down?"

"Great! That's settled then, we'll order you a car to come around our office on Monday, well ahead of the US launch. Now, about this wine!"

Process, not Event

It was Monday, the day of the Zillian IPO. Cat, along with Lottie and Tessa had just arrived at the Triangle Offices.

Clare, Jake, Bigsy and Christina were already in a meeting room.

Jake spoke, "Welcome, Cat, I think you know some of us, but we'll all introduce ourselves. Then for our education and sanity it would be good if you could explain the process to us."

Formalities over, Cat began, "Having an IPO is not so much an event as it is a process. It takes months of planning to prepare a company to go public. A board of directors must be assembled, accounts audited for accuracy, consultants and advisers hired. In fact, a whole cast of characters must take the stage to help an IPO happen."

Cat continued, "The most important character is probably the underwriter, an investment banker who works for an investment company. Our company - the one for which I work - will sometimes be involved in getting underwriters allocated."

"But you use other people to provide the actual money and investment?" checked Bigsy.

"Yes, that's right. Underwriters have the distribution channels and business community contacts that can get a company's shares out to the right investors.

"They will also help set the initial offering price for the stocks, work to create enthusiasm for the stock, and assist in creating the prospectus. The prospectus is an important document that describes the company in detail to potential investors. Once the prospectus has been drafted, it is reviewed by the SEC."

"That's a big deal, to ensure that the IPO is legitimate?" asked Jake.

Cat answered, " Kind of. SEC approval only means that the prospectus follows the regulations for such documents -- it says nothing about the quality or future profitability of the company. When I looked at Zillian, it had the aura of something just 'too good to be true'!"

"As we also thought!" said Jake.

Cat continued, "Following SEC approval, company executives go onto a road show, otherwise known as the dog-and-pony show. This is a tour of major cities and cities where important brokerage houses have their headquarters."

"I think we had our share of those events in Switzerland!" said Lottie.

Cat continued, "At these invitation-only slide shows, potential investors are given "goodie bags" containing trinkets elaborating the company's product, and whatever else might help investors think favourably about the company."

"So that's where all the toy cars came from!" said Tessa, laughing.

"We were having a competition to see who could get the most, but then we realised they were quite heavy in our luggage," explained Lottie.

Cat continued with the briefing, "The road-show crew also includes a tame Wall Street analyst who will give positive opinions about the company's future profitability. However, no one involved with the company is allowed to talk publicly about anything that isn't in the prospectus in the period leading up to the IPO."

"I think Google got caught out with something like that," muttered Jake, "Something about a Playboy article..." His words trailed away, "I can't believe I just said that out loud,"

Cat smiled, "You are right about that article, by the way. Then, the day before the stocks are issued, the underwriter and the company must determine a starting price for the stocks. It is what they have done with Zillian."

"But it isn't the same as the target price?" asked Jake.

Cat nodded, "Quite right, a target price will have been set early in the process, but IPOs are rarely stable. Obviously, the higher the price, the more money the company gets; but if the price is set too high, there won't be enough demand for the stocks, and the price will drop on the aftermarket."

Then she added, "The ideal stock price will keep demand just higher than supply, resulting in a stable, gradual increase in the stock's price on the aftermarket. This will lead to praise from market analysts, which will in turn lead to increased value down the road."

"Peachy," said Jake, "But can anyone buy shares in an IPO?"

Cat answered, "Not really. Who gets to buy the shares during an IPO is a complicated matter. In most cases, your typical, individual investor doesn't get access to these offerings. Instead, the underwriter gets to allocate the shares to associates, clients, and major investors of his choosing. In effect it is a closed shop."

"So, what type of people get the shares?" asked Clare.

Cat answered, "Most of the shares - up to 80 percent -will go to institutional investors, typically it is major brokerage firms and investment banks, and a few high-profile individual investors. And, by the way, in this case it looks as if Brant are one of them.

Cat explained, "After the initial offering, the stocks hit the open stock market, where they begin trading at a price set by market forces. IPO stocks tend to trade at a very high volume on that first day -- that is, they change hands many times. Some IPOs can jump in price by a huge amount -- some more than 600 percent. However, many IPOs do poorly, dropping in price the day of the offering. Others fluctuate, rising and then dipping again -- it all depends on the confidence the market has in the company, how strong the company is vs. the hype surrounding it, and what outside forces are affecting the market at the time."

Shea added, "I'd be very surprised if Zillian went up because of the window dressing around their numbers which will put many people off."

"So, this doesn't look very promising for our two MPs?" asked Clare.

"Not on Day 1," answered Cat, "But after about a month, the underwriter issues a report on the IPO, which is always positive. This tends to give the stock a slight boost. After 180 days have passed, people who held shares in the company prior to its going public are allowed to sell their shares."

"But why would I want to sell shares, if they haven't done very well?" asked Jake.

"Well, if I was given the initial money to buy the shares, that could be one reason," answered Cat, "Although I might be better off hanging in there if I knew that an uplift was likely,"

"Precisely, " said Christina, "Firstly, If the MPs and other inner core of shareholders know that some good news is coming. Secondly, if the investment has been hidden in a tax haven."

"What? So, no-one knows about the investments?" asked Bigsy.

"Exactly!" said Cat.

"Then it is truly a magic money tree!" said Jake.

Bigsy had rigged up a stock ticker for the share in the office. It blinked on the launch price. "ZILL $17.00"

"Is that a good launch price?" asked Clare.

"It is almost impossible for me to say," answered Cat, "There are a few other car companies to compare with, but they are each their own self-contained valuation. It'd be like trying to compare two bank share prices. For example, Lloyds Bank shares at 52p and HSBC Bank valued at £5.59, some ten times larger. By itself the figure means very little."

"I can see that with Tesla," said Clare, "It ran at $50 for years - but then spiked up to nearly $1000."

"Exactly," said Cat, "And that must be what the Zillian inner-core shareholders are hoping too. Presumably on the back of good news announced by those two MPs!"

They all looked at the ticker, trading had started, but the ZILL price was now $16.52.

"It doesn't look like a mover and shaker, " announced Jake, "And after all of this effort!"

They watched and the price moved to ZILL $17.22.

"Hmm, that's a 1% increase!" said Bigsy.

The price fell back to $17.14.

"It looks as if the initial take-up of the offered shares was what set the original price. The later trading isn't making much of an impression," said Cat.

"We'll need to see what tomorrow and the next 4 weeks bring," said Cat, "Of course those MPs can cash out after a month and still get their tax-free $1 million each."

Unbelievable

You burden me with your questions
You'd have me tell no lies
You're always asking what it's all about
But don't listen to my replies
You say to me I don't talk enough
But when I do, I'm a fool
These times I've spent, I've realised
I'm going to shoot through and leave you

The things you say
Your purple prose just gives you away
The things you say
You're unbelievable

You burden me with your problems
By telling me more than mine
I'm always so concerned
With the way you say you always have to stop
To think of us being one
Is more than I ever know
But this time, I realize
I'm going to shoot through and leave you
The things you say
Your purple prose just gives you away

You burden me with your questions
You'd have me tell no lies
You're always asking what it's all about
But don't listen to my replies
You say to me I don't talk enough
But when I do, I'm a fool

Dench | Atkin | Brownson | Decloedt | Foley

You're Undetectable

The next morning, Bigsy was reading a news feed:

FINANCE WORLD NEWS

In February, Red Fox Capital — a special-purpose acquisition company (SPAC) — announced a deal to take automobile manufacturers Zillian public, valuing the company at $8 billion. The company is going public "to accelerate into the next phase of our growth," Zillian CEO Miller McDonald said.

A SPAC, also known as a blank-cheque company, is an alternative to a traditional initial public offering. These blank-cheque companies have no assets beyond cash. They trade on stock exchanges and then merge with private companies, taking those companies public.

Zillian began trading under the ticker symbol ZILL on the Nasdaq.

Zillian started delivering its Zillian 502 — a high-performance, ultra-efficient luxury EV sedan four months ago, according to the company. The company expects to roll out its Zillion 602 performance luxury SUV within the next year. The Zillion 302 started in production a month ago.

In a slide deck filed with the U.S. Securities and Exchange Commission Zillian Motors touted more than 10,000 reservations for the Zillian 302, representing $700 million in anticipated sales. It claimed the 302 beats the Tesla Model S and Amazon-backed EV startup Rivian's R1T in battery efficiency, which it calls the ultimate measure of EV technology. It also claims the Zillian 302 beats luxury EVs from Jaguar, Porsche, and Audi on that metric.

Zillian touts EV technology it developed in-house. It describes the Zillian 302 as the 'quickest, longest-range, fastest-charging electric car in the world,' delivering 500 miles of range.

The Environmental Protection Agency hasn't certified that range yet. The 302 also boasts high-end features such as a 'glass cockpit.' The Zillian 302 features an autonomous driving system using 32 sensors, including long-distance Lidar, a safety technology that Tesla long avoided.

The first fully loaded 302 will cost around $160,000, including federal subsidies. Cheaper versions will be released, with a $70,000 version expected within a year.

ZILL Stock Technical Analysis

According to the IBD Stock Checkup, ZILL shows a weak 30 out of a perfect 99 IBD Composite Rating. The Composite Rating helps investors easily measure a stock's fundamental and technical metrics. Weak IBD Composite Ratings are normal for new issues.

The SEC could be alerted to the unusually intense buying and selling of Zillian shares following the IPO. Conventionally, the short-term profit taking is frowned upon for a new company launch.

Zillian Motors Stock News

Before the IPO, Zillian Motors shareholders voted to approve the merger of the blank check company.

The company said it had finished its preproduction phase after a series of delays. "The testing and validation of Zillian 302 is progressing well," CEO Miller McDonald said on the call. "It's on track for the start of production for customer deliveries."

"This all looks pretty direct for investors," said Bigsy, "one car produced in limited numbers and another couple on the way. The share price was hijacked by shot term traders in for a quick buck and now the share price is floundering round its original launch level."

"I agree," said Jake, "Except that people who invested dirty money can still pull out clean money, and in the case of those MPs there isn't even taxation to worry about."

"Yes," said Clare, "It's tantamount to a massive dirty bribe to both Melship and Tovey, in return for which they will boost the value of the Zillian shares."

"Mega-sleaze, " said Bigsy.

"And almost undetectable," added Jake.

Infrastructure Improvement Committee Session

Matt Stevens and Lottie Trevethick had been asked to support Michael Tovey and Duncan Melship at an upcoming Infrastructure Improvement Committee Session.

"Hmm, this is awkward," said Matt, as his arm grazed Lottie's shoulder on the way into the session."

"Only as difficult as you want to make it," returned Lottie.

Humphrey Morris (Conservative, Brampton and Blissett) brought the committee to order. There were eleven MPs present, and Lottie only recognised a couple beyond Melship and Tovey. She realised that as an Assistant, she was invisible to most of the MPs, except the patently lecherous one who was eyeing her rather too intently.

Matt whispered, "I think you have a follower," into Lottie's ear, which helped her decide she would sit elsewhere in the room.

The Committee rumbled into a discussion of Levelling Up, a topic only known to Sonic the Hedgehog gamers until it became political capital. The phrase "levelling up" had steadily proliferated across Whitehall, and the committee was expecting a landmark "levelling up white paper."

Ahead of that publication, MPs published a report concluding that the concept 'has yet to be defined', adding to widespread narrative that 'levelling up' is an empty political slogan.

"Oh dear," thought Lottie, "this committee will need light speed shoes, crystal rings and a bounce bracelet to get out of this conundrum."

Then, one of the MPs Robert Bighampton (Conservative, East Pagentree), presented a levelling up example based upon the Humber Bridge, which connects Hull with the East Midlands. It commenced construction in 1966 and opened to traffic in 1981.

It cost £385 million to build at 2021 prices. It was financed by Government loans, which accrued interest. Those loans have yet to be fully repaid despite a toll being levied on bridge users. In 2012, former Chancellor of the Exchequer George Osborne reduced toll charges on the bridge from £3 to £1.50 each way for cars and removed motorcycle tolls. The lower tolls were introduced following the Government's writing down almost 50% of the outstanding £330 million.

"This is before levelling up was a thing," thought Lottie, "Surely they can't be trying to claim it?"

The presenter droned on, "According to the Infrastructure and Projects Authority's (IPA's) Annual Report on Major Projects 2020–21, major projects on the Government Major Projects Portfolio are 'typically those where approval is required from The Treasury, either because the budget exceeds a department's delegated authority level and/or because the project is novel, complex, contentious, or requires primary legislation'.

"Although the bridge reduced journey times for the local population and connected families and businesses, it did not produce tangible economic returns."

"Yes, and today, Hull has one of the highest unemployment rates in the country," thought Lottie.

The presenter added, "The Department awaits the Government's forthcoming Levelling Up White Paper' which must clarify how major transport infrastructure projects can contribute to levelling up."

'We are all stuck in the glue of an enormous machine, ' thought Lottie, 'Where every report and its conclusions is dependent upon something else.

Only a few projects escape to conclusion, and if they are like Humber Bridge, then the results are not altogether conclusive. It becomes a great place to hide anything.'

The presenter continued, "The Department plans to develop proposals for the 'robust assessment and presentation of distributional and place- based impacts to support decision makers in better understanding impacts on priorities such as levelling up'.

'Jargon-central,' thought Lottie, tapping notes on her iPad.

"It is also reviewing its "rebalancing toolkit" and wider strategic case guidance to correspond with the latest updates to the Green Book. If those reviews are to be meaningful, the Department will need to define the "levelling up" policy agenda in a transport context to set a benchmark against which to test business cases.

Lottie thought again, 'A rebalancing toolkit! It sounds as if something is being developed, but it could just as easily be a playpen activity designed to obfuscate.'

Then the Presenter added, "To allow Parliament and the public to judge the effectiveness of the Government's infrastructure plans, the Government must publish detailed metrics that define and measure the 'levelling up' concept.

"We are concerned that the Department did not explain how the construction of major transport infrastructure projects can support the 'levelling up' policy agenda. We would be reassured if the Department were to set out a worked example illustrating how investment in major transport infrastructure projects drives growth and productivity."

'Oh yes,' thought Lottie, 'After we've just seen an example of a project which built a bridge, didn't recover its costs and still the area of the UK is one of the poorest. It makes a great case for levelling up.'

The committee moved on, under the guidance of Humphrey Morris, who thanked Robert Bighampton and moved on to discuss costs and timescales. Sarah Blackburn (Labour, Kingston Turnberry) stood to present the HS2 costings.

"It's a simple case study," she began: "The first estimates for the cost of HS2 were published in the February 2011 HS2 economic case. Phase One costs were estimated to be £19.6 billion, with the full network estimated at £37.5 billion. Phase One from London to Birmingham is now estimated to cost between £31 billion and £40 billion, an increase of between 14% and 47% from the £27.1 billion funding allocated in 2013."

'A mighty increase,' thought Lottie, 'but it is difficult to pick through strings of recited numbers like this. A couple of charts would be better.'

Sarah Blackburn continued, "A target cost for Phase One has been set at £36 billion, or £40 billion in 2019 prices. Originally due to open in 2026, the full opening of the Phase One into Euston station is now expected between 2031 and 2036, although services from Old Oak Common are due to commence between 2029 and 2033."

'They've published two completion dates; it'll be the last one with more added slippage,' thought Lottie, 'Instead of 2026, its seven years later at double the cost.'

Sarah Blackburn continued, "The estimated cost of Phase 2a has also increased from £3.5 billion in 2013 at 2015 prices, to between £4.5 billion and £6.5 billion, an increase of between 29% and 87%."

'It will be over 100% cost increase and take years longer. Burn rate is a consultancy's friend,' thought Lottie.

Sarah Blackburn added, "Phase 2a is now due to open between 2030 and 2031, three to four years later than expected. The cost of Phase 2b is now estimated to be between £29 billion and £41 billion, an increase of between 15% and 63% on the £25 billion previously allocated in 2013, and three to seven years behind schedule. The current estimate is for services to open between 2036 and 2040, compared with the original target date of 2033."

'Hilarious, if it wasn't so gross,' thought Lottie, 'Now they will be blaming the original estimates for being wrong. Estimates which they were put under political pressure to provide within certain parameters.'

Sarah Blackburn added, "Those statistics suggest that initial costs and timescales were not properly assessed. The various Ministers with responsibility for HS2 who signed off those estimates have not been held to account for their miscalculations at taxpayers' expense."

'Nor will they,' thought Lottie.

Humphrey Morris stood, thanked Sarah Blackburn, and called Duncan Melship.

'Light blue touchpaper, ' thought Lottie, 'now for fireworks.'

Fireworks

Duncan Melship began.

Lottie realised he was speaking from a well-worn talk track that he used when presenting to schools and general citizen briefings.

"The government sets the objectives and funding for Highways England through a periodic Road Investment Strategy (RIS), which covers a five-year Road Period.

"The first RIS was published in 2014 and applied to the first Road Period, 2015 to 2020. RIS2 was published in March 2020 and applied to the second Road Period, 2020 to 2025. We are now gathering evidence to inform RIS3, which will apply to the Road Period starting in 2025.

"During this first Road Period we:
- Started work on 67 major road schemes, opening 36, with 21 of these schemes opening ahead of schedule.

- Stayed within our funding agreement.
- Delivered £1.4 billion of efficiencies.
- Provided £2.50 of public benefit for every £1 we spent on our major schemes.
- Made the SRN safer and reduced casualties in line with our ambitious targets to cut the number of people killed or seriously injured on our network by 40%.
- Invested over £650 million in projects which have reduced noise, alleviated flooding, protected biodiversity, reduced air pollution, and provided alternative routes for walkers and cyclists. This includes 113 safety schemes, 160 cycling schemes, 124 biodiversity schemes and 1174 noise mitigation schemes: and
- Improved how we work with our supply chain, creating new commercial models, driving efficiency savings, investment, and innovations. In April 2020, we entered the second Road Period and we started to deliver RIS2. We are investing £27.4 billion into England's Strategic Road Network over the next five years."

Lottie thought, 'Melship is making his department seem on-the-ball after the prior two presentations.'

She waited for the Big Ask from Melship. First, he described the Strategic Road Network and its important social role, bringing people together and connecting communities and regions.

Then, "As a key infrastructure delivery partner of the government, our plans for this second Road Period (2020-2025) and beyond will see us play an important role in realising the priority outcomes set out in the NIS. Our operation, maintenance, and improvement of the SRN over the next five years and beyond will support:

- Rebuilding the economy.
- Setting a new carbon-light agenda for roads in the Capital.
- Procurement of exclusively carbon-light government vehicles, from preferred and reliable suppliers.
- Supporting the government's 'levelling-up' agenda by connecting all parts of the country, the Union, and provision of better access to international gateways in support of trade.
- Decarbonisation and adapting to climate change.
- Delivering better infrastructure more efficiently; and
- Protecting and enhancing the environment.

"In its second Road Investment Strategy (RIS2) published in March 2020, the government set out its vision for a safer, more reliable, and greener SRN that uses new technology, supports the country's economy, and is an integrated part of the national transport network. Our Departmental aims are in support of this vision."

Melship looked across to Humphrey Morris, who stood thanked Duncan Melship and moved toward the next Agenda item. "But before we do that, I think we all deserve a break!"

'There,' thought Lottie, 'He has said it. Buried in a Committee speech. Two bullets built into the next Strategic Road Network Plan, which give Zillian their keys to the British economy, and give Melship and Tovey around £1 million each.'

China

China all the way to New York
I can feel the distance getting close
You're right next to me
But I need an airplane
I can feel the distance as you breathe
Sometimes I think you want me to touch you
How can I when you build a great wall around you
In your eyes I saw a future together
You just look away in the distance
China decorates our table
Funny how the cracks don't seem to show
Pour the wine dear
You say we'll take a holiday
But we never can agree on where to go
Sometimes I think you want me to touch you
How can I when you build a great wall around you
In your eyes I saw a future together
You just look away in the distance
China all the way to New York
Maybe you got lost in Mexico
You're right next to me
I think that you can hear me
Funny how the distance learns to grow
Sometimes I think you want me to touch you
How can I when you build a great wall around you
I can feel the distance
I can feel the distance
I can feel the distance getting close

Tori Ellen Amos

700 per cent

The session continued in the Committee Room for another three hours. It was almost 5 pm when they broke and Lottie was back online.

She and Matt were both immediately greeted with a torrent of messages. She wondered what could be so important, but as soon as she opened the first message she realised.

Zillian had run a press announcement the same afternoon as Melship's speech. Whilst he and Tovey were locked away in committee, Zillian had announced their deal with the UK Government. The UK was to procure up to 10,000 vehicles from Zillian and additionally was declaring that most of Greater London would become a petrol and diesel-free zone.

Both Melship and Tovey had finely crafted press statements extolling the virtues of these decisions and the Prime Minister appeared to be in on the process too, virtue signalling that the UK would be the first major nations to deliver an ecologically positive set of reforms.

Lottie checked one of the monitors inside the Commons. A TV show from London Today was running and showed a hubbub around Parliament's gates and another one outside Downing Street. This was the story of the day. The opposition were finding it difficult to be critical because it is something that they had theoretically promoting for the last few years.

At this rate, Melship and Tovey could come through this looking like political heroes, and the Prime Minister would be tugging at their coattails to get profile-enhancing draught.

Lottie wondered about the ZILL share price. It had been around $17.50 the last time she had looked. She gasped when she clicked it on her phone. $122.53. A rise of some 700%. Zillian shares had rocketed on the combined news. And it would also mean that Melship and Tovey had earned a cool and undetectable £6million extra during that Committee session. Something like £1 million per hour, and no tax to worry about.

Lottie called Clare.

"Have you seen it?" she asked, "Oh yes," said Clare, "We are all looking at it now. Zillian has turned from a cheeky ape into an 800-lb gorilla."

Clare continued, "Bigsy asked us: 'Where does an 800-pound gorilla sit?' and you know the answer:

'Anywhere it wants to.' "

"I was called by Amanda Miller as well," said Clare, "She wants to put a stop to this. I've never heard her sound angry, but she did this time."

"Shall we pay her a visit?" asked Lottie, "I was in Melship and Tovey's committee meeting."

"Good idea," said Clare.

Generous donors

Amanda Miller usually worked from the Thames location of the SIS-(MI6) building based at 85 Albert Embankment, Vauxhall Cross.

For this meeting, she opted to cross the river to the MI5 building at Thames House, situated on Millbank and only a short walk from the Houses of Parliament.

"I wonder why we are meeting here?" asked Clare.

Bigsy shrugged his shoulders.

Jake answered, "Well, she has plenty of sites to choose from, I suppose."

Clare, Bigsy, Jake and Christina also knew about the other Secret Service buildings spread around London. One in the Square Mile of the City, a network control centre on the 17th floor of Euston

Tower and a spy training school in South London. A few buildings had been closed too, notably Kennington Lane, with its bubble doors like the ones in the TV-show Spooks and the old GCHQ building in Palmer Street.

Bigsy explained, "It's always good to look for a BT Openreach Monitoring Station, if you want to know where the secret services are operating. There's one by Parliament, another by the Stock Exchange, one in the City close to the Bank of England and then there's that whole warren around Holborn in the West End."

"I thought the big tunnels under Holborn and Kingsway were used for something else?" queried Clare.

"Monitoring of individuals," answered Bigsy, "Both landline and cellular,"

"Are we really living in a police state?" asked Jake.

"Well monitored, but you've seen how the Met has been perceived," answered Bigsy, "but I doubt we will ever find out what really happened."

Christina smiled, "It not just the UK that monitors in London. The US, the Kremlin and the Chinese have listening posts too.

"I sometimes wonder with all those phones and ancillary communications manufactured in China," said Bigsy, "How difficult would it be to add a few backdoors?"

Amanda appeared, with Grace.

"Oh ladies, this is indeed an honour to have you both here, in person, I have such memories of this place!" said Jake.

Amanda smiled, "Jake, Ah yes, when we had to lock you up in this building a few years ago!"

"But you let him out, when we returned from Arizona!" smiled Clare.

"Okay," said Amanda, "I used this building for a good reason. It is far easier to bring Members of Parliament here, than it is to take them across the River. It could be a simple security matter here; over the water it implies dealing with foreign agents."

"So, who have you got locked up this time?" asked Jake.

"It has to be Melship or Tovey," said Christina, "I'd go for just one of them, probably Tovey to exert the most pain," said Christina.

"Christina, you are right. Although we have Duncan Melship held in the Annex, with Lottie Trevethick."

"What is the angle?" asked Jake.

"We need to put a stop to the Zillian plan. Melship is going to help us," answered Amanda.

Grace flicked on a presentation.

"Here we are: Melship with Miller McDonald, Mary Ranzino, Qiu Zhang and Volvakov Kirill Valeryevich. And in the background is the Zillian logo."

Jake spoked, "Yes, but that's circumstantial? Can't prove anything from the group of them standing by a car stand at an exhibition."

"I agree," said Grace, "but we are building a picture."

She moved to the next slide. It showed a transaction. Banca Cariba, in the name of Duncan Melship. A deposit of £1 million.

"Where on earth did you get that?" asked Jake.

"We were very lucky," answered Grace, "Let's say a recent friend of Matt Stevens helped us."

"Charlotte Mendez?" said Christina, "I thought there was something unusual about her sudden relationship with Matt."

"Correct," said Grace, "Our associate Charlotte had to persuade Matt that it was simplest for Tovey to bank with Banca Cariba. He did and then persuaded Melship to do the same."

"It was so simple for them to open their Banca Cariba accounts with no tax returns in an offshore tax haven."

"So, you have got a similar sword hanging over Tovey?" asked Christina.

"Yes, but we don't want to reveal that part yet, especially because it will illustrate Matt Stevens' gullibility. This way it looks like an unfortunate circumstance."

"Em, this is delicate, but it looks as if the Prime Minister may also be involved in some of this," said Clare, "He and his immediately surrounding Cabinet of Ministers seem to have turned a blind eye to way that the original deal for Zillian was passed by the Commons, without any difficult questions."

"The PM is a friend of Miller McDonald. He has provided the Tory Party with some immense donations in the past," answered Grace. "According to press sources just 10 wealthy people account for a quarter of all donations made by individuals to the Conservative Party."

"But how much?" asked Jake.

Grace continued, "The 10 super-rich donors – nine of whom are men – have given a combined sum of just over £10m to the Tories equalling more than 25 per cent of the £38.6m received from all individuals in the past two years."

Jake added, "I know it is a lot of money, but somehow, in the scheme of this Zillian scam, it doesn't seem so much to pay to be in control of the direction of the United Kingdom."

Grace added, "Yes. Fears have been expressed about the power held by the very wealthiest Tory donors after it emerged that a group known as the Advisory Board had been developed to connect the party's biggest financial backers with ministers."

Grace continued, "One of the 10 most generous donors is Miller McDonald, CEO of Brant Industries, who has given almost £1,000,000 to the Tory party in the last two years. MacDonald's ties with the Tories came under scrutiny earlier this year when it emerged his company was a co-investor in a failed bid to buy a Premier league football team."

"That could be an interesting additional source of money laundering," mused Clare.

Grace added, "Other wealthy Tory donors on the top 10 list include an online trading tycoon who has given the party just over £870,000 in the past two years. He was handed a peerage last year – sparking accusations of cronyism from Labour. It is rumoured that Miller McDonald is also in line for a peerage."

"But I thought Miller McDonald was American?" asked Bigsy, "I mean he sounds American when he speaks?"

Grace answered, "No. Miller McDonald is actually British - Scottish to be precise. He hails from

Braemar, which is quite close to the Royal residence at Balmoral. It means he is free to donate to the party and can bag a peerage when the party shows sufficient gratitude."

"I guess that is after several years of consistent donations?" said Jake, "I remember Street - that's my old magazine - did an article once about Quintessentially, a luxury concierge service, which offered (among other things) to connect Tory donors to senior figures - like the Prime Minister and the Chancellor. I suspect the so-called Advisory Board was copied from that idea."

"Well, we should bring Duncan Melship into play now," said Amanda, "Although I'm going to run that session from another interview room. You'll all be outside, but still able to see what happens. And Grace, you'd better come with me."

Grace flicked a few buttons and a different scene appeared from the projector. It was of a small interview room, like the ones used in TV police interviews, but with slightly more opulent furniture.

"They won't be able to hear you," said Grace, "although you'll be able to hear everything."

Free-for-all?

Bigsy, Clare, Jake and Christina watched, as Douglas Melship and Lottie appeared in the new interview room. Then Amanda and Grace walked in, along with a third, suited and rather serious looking man."

"It's Jim Cavendish," said Clare, "Amanda is bringing in the big guns for this meeting."

Cavendish was Amanda's boss and they had known one another for many years.

"Another reason to pick this side of the River," said Jake, "Jim can do a drop in for the interview."

Jim opened the session.

"Douglas! It must be three years since we last met, how time flies!"

"Hello James, yes it has been a while, and look at you now, a centre Chief here at MI5!"

"That's right, I get involved when there seems to be a major situation developing."

"Not one with me, I hope?" said Melship.

"Well, yes, actually. You seem have stumbled into something quite big. It could even be considered as a plot to overthrow the government."

"It must be some kind of mix-up," answered Melship, "I've done nothing out of the ordinary, my life continues on its usual routine way."

"Not quite, said Jim, "We can see you are mixed up with this company called Zillian. You even recommended them in the House to be a UK supplier of vehicles."

"Well, it was after the usual due-diligence, James,"

"Was it Duncan? I mean, you seem to like the company so much you had shares in it?"

"No, I don't think so," said Melship.

"Curious then, that we found your offshore account where you'd purchased almost £1 million of Zillian shares,"

"No, it must be some mistake, to be handling such a large quantity and just before that announcement from the UK Government that it would be investing in Zillian? You spoke to the House and even had the

Prime Minister later signing the deal's praises."

"I don't recollect any stake holding in the company and I'm sure I will have followed all government guidelines on any investments."

"Well, that is a relief, someone else must have planted that money offshore and used your name to attempt to hide it, otherwise it would be ruinous to you, both financially and reputationally."

"Something else has come to light too, about Zillian."

Those watching could all see that Melship wasn't the best at hiding his concerns.

"He is wriggling, " said Christina, "Can't take the pressure of being found out. Classic lack of interrogation experience."

Jake and Bigsy laughed, Christian was viewing this with her professional eye.

"Grace, I think you'd better show Duncan here what else we have discovered,"

Grace pulled up a couple of line drawings of cars.

"It's the Zillian 302, and next to it is the Lotya M300, which is built as an electric taxicab in Hangzhou, China. The two cars are identical, right down to the Wanzijiang Group manufactured battery cells. Same length, width, height, wheelbase, weight and stated performance."

Melship was looking at the car as if it was the first time he had seen one.

Grace continued, "Look I found a couple of photos too, they are almost indistinguishable from one another."

Then she flipped to another picture. It showed a road accident.

"This is one of the Lotya M300s on fire. The battery pack overheated. Fortunately, the driver and passenger were able to get out and walk to safety."

Amanda spoke now, "Due to the incident, the Hangzhou city authorities decided to halt all electric taxis on safety concerns. Fifteen of them were Lotya M300 EVs out of a fleet of 30 electric taxis."

Melship looked surprised to hear this, but he had also looked surprised to see one of the Zillian 302s in the earlier picture.

Grace started again, "The city's official investigation team found the cause of the fire was the car's defective battery pack due to lack of quality control during manufacturing. According to the investigation report, the battery pack problems include leaking of battery cells; damage of the insulation between battery cells and the walls of the aluminium container in which the cells were stacked; short circuits occurred within certain containers and those involving supporting and connecting parts."

She added, "One of the stronger short circuits ignited the car's back seats. The lead investigators said that '...in sealing and packing the battery cells, in loading and unloading the battery stacks, insufficient attention had been paid to several safety factors; monitoring procedures had been inefficient or neglected in the process of manufacturing, battery charging/switching, and vehicle driving, failing to detect anomalies.'

Amanda spoke, "The report added that the battery cells on the car were made by Wanzijiang Group."

Jim continued, "Okay Duncan, we can see that one occurrence would be an unlucky event; even Tesla had some early problems with their first Roadster in 2006. There were some thermal issues when accelerating fast and pushing the car to its limits. Clearly, a risk of fire or overheating is not something which Tesla was looking for when developing an electric car which would prove the technology to the world.

Grace picked up the description: "Consequently, Tesla developed the Battery Management System (BMS), a system which is still used as a similar design in the Model S, 3 and X today."

She added, "Whatever type of BMS Tesla uses, it needs to be powerful to cool all of the 7000 battery cells. Tesla patented a battery cooling system for the Model S which allowed each of the cells to make contact with a coolant pipe."

Then Jim Cavendish again, "Now the difference with EV car fires is the use of high voltage lithium-ion batteries which can short, break down and spontaneously combust, and also that lithium-ion fires both are difficult to extinguish and produce thick toxic smoke."

Grace continued, "The running temperature of an EV is perfect for short, peak performance like rapid accelerations and top speed runs. Subsequently, the battery pack must be both heated and cooled to create the perfect temperature range. This is done with the BMS (battery management system)."

Jake spoke from the monitor room, "Melship looks as if he needs a Battery Management System." Tell-tale beads of sweat had broken out across Melship's forehead.

Grace continued, "Furthermore, when the V3 superchargers were released, a new Model 3 setting was engaged which would allow batteries to be 'preconditioned' before receiving maximum charging speeds. This preconditioning will include heating or cooling to get the battery to about 30 degrees Celsius or a little more for superfast charging. It is a clever design and must add considerably to the manufacturing costs of the vehicle. Any equivalent design is notably absent from the Zillian 302 EV and the Lotya M300 EV."

"And Melship," said Bigsy.

Grace continued, "We decided to dig further. We found that the designs of the next two Zillian cars were based upon clone cars manufactured in China. Both the Zillian 502 and the 602 are copies of Chinese car models. None of the ones copied had any form of BMS. There were no statistics for the Zillian's safety record, but we substituted their original close cars to get a safety breakdown.

Grace continued, "It was truly shocking. For the 302, there were 137 fires: for the 502 another 22 fires and for the limited production 602 another 8 fires. These statistics were eared across a large area of China and it may because of this that the trend had not been identified."

Jim again, "Our conclusion? The cars are not safe and the fires generated - of a chemical nature - are huge pollutants."

Douglas Melship looked towards Lottie as if asking her to say something. It was clear that his time in Gstaad hadn't given him a grasp of the technology.

Lottie asked, "But won't that make our government look awkward. We've just agreed, in principle, to procure 10,000 of these Zillian cars and vans?"

"Yes, but we have already sought legal advice and are to cancel the contact. It's called Rescission.

Jim continued, "And if we have to cite anything, then it will be the ultimate safety of the vehicles being provided. That the ones offered did not have suitable built-in safety features and that the manufacturer did not have sufficient oversight of the production process."

Melship spoke again, "But what will this do to the share prices of Zillian?"

Jim answered, "I should think it will destroy it, but they are selling a worthless product and are a company that cannot be trusted."

"And the effect upon the Prime Minister?"

Jim answered, "Well, it is no secret that he is already on shaky ground. He can tough this out and re-invent the storyline, but fundamentally, he must have gone into this with his eyes opened, perhaps with an eye upon the next big donation from Miller McDonald. I think you should ask about yourself too, I'd imagine your reputation in government will be in tatters after this, and I suspect that your 'investment' with Banca Cariba will have dwindled away."

"When will this all happen, the cancellation of the contract, I mean?"

"Today. It has already occurred. You are very lucky that we have cancelled for cause. It means you are not directly implicated. You will have kept your side of the bargain with Zillian and Red Fox so they should not feel the need for revenge."

"And what about Tovey?" asked Melship.

Jim answered, "He knows even less about what has happened. Zillian will go to him first, but it will be obvious that he knows nothing. Unless you tell him, of course, although that would be mighty stupid. I shall leave you now, Mr Melship."

Jim rose to leave the room.

"Wow," said Bigsy, "He doesn't mess around."

Bigsy looked at the ZILL ticker on his iPhone, "The ZILL share has dropped 26% since start of trading. It is still going down."

Clare's phone rang. It was Cat.

"What have you done?" she asked, "Only Zillian's share price is crashing. The guys around here say it is a dead man walking. It has just been suspended from trading. That's like it has just hit an iceberg and is about to do a long-drawn-out Titanic. It will ripple through to the political forums too, they are saying."

Bigsy asked, "But it is still working here?"

Cat replied, "Trust me. It is dead, your feed must have a 15-minute delay."

Amanda and Grace re-entered the room, "You've heard?" asked Amanda, "The Shares have been suspended?"

Grace flicked the presentation screen to display a news channel.

Christina looked at the screen, still showing the interview room. "It's all been too simple," she said, "I think there is still some other play out there."

Clare summarised,

- "Car firm inflates its share price through tricks."
- "Chinese and Russians invest in leveraged deal - smaller money invested but bigger returns"
- "They blackmail, coerce and bribe two MPs to talk up the share price"
- "Share goes up, and China/Russia make money on covert markets."
- "Car firm discovered as a sham."
- "MPs challenged and deny knowledge"
- "Car firm crashes because of discoveries."
- "Car firm suspended - is worth nothing."

"There is your key window," said Christina, "When the share price rose, all the hidden money could be moved and cashed. That's the money laundering part, but it was so short lived. It has to be a diversion for something else."

The television was running implications of the failure of Zillian and the embarrassment to the UK Government, where the Prime Minister himself had backed the investment. Then it cut to a UK map. It showed several UK locations, designated as Freeports.

The narrator continued to explain their use.

"That's it," said Christina, "They've used the potential import of Zillian cars to secure two of the UK Freeports. Thames and Freeport East. If all of those cars were to have been imported on container ships, they would have needed somewhere to land."

She added, "You watch, even if Zillian gets cancelled, those Freeports will survive."

Grace nodded agreement, "Yes, a white paper for the Centre for Policy Studies outlined ideas for post-Brexit free ports like those in the United States. The paper titled The Free Ports Opportunity suggested that creation of such ports could create 86,000 jobs and help fuel the Northern Powerhouse by bringing increased trade to deprived areas.

"That's the other play," said Christina, "Most of what we've seen was a decoy manoeuvre, but it has secured the Free Ports and has let through the legislation to create them as casinos for the rich and powerful. Deregulation of the tax base, aimed at facilitating tax havens, smuggling and removal of worker's rights."

Clare spoke, "No wonder the Prime Minister didn't look too upset."

"Nor the Pomps and the hyphenated," added Jake, "It will become a free-for-all!"

Wrap up

Jake, Bigsy, Clare and Christina were all in a wine bar within some railway vaults. Jake had invited Rachel but urged her to remain off duty. Lottie, Hannah, and Tessa had been invited and were intrigued to see sawdust scattered on the floor.

"How should we feel about this? Did we learn anything?" asked Clare.

"I wish we'd spotted it earlier, " said Christina, "You know; the real game was to create the Freeports which can be exploited like giant casinos by the Russians and Chinese."

"And certain UK politicians," added Bigsy.

"David, my brother, was on to them and paid with his life, " added Rachel, "I'm so glad you have found out what they were doing and have brought some of them down."

"The Russians and Chinese managed to launder

money through Zillian before it went belly-up," added Jake, "But slow-moving Melship and Tovey saw their shares go up and then crash again."

"These Russians were being run by bratva gangs, " added Christina, "they are utterly ruthless, and now the Chinese are starting to copy them. Isabella and then Douglas both killed. It even got the Kremlin agitated, although I suspect it was partly in case any of Putin's secrets were about to be revealed."

"But he's covered his tracks," said Bigsy, "Unlike the Brits involved in all of this."

"The Brits won't ever learn about how to cover their tracks fully," said Christina, "It was too easy to find those two MP accounts in Banca Cariba."

Jake said, "They are both finished as MPs now, though, with corruption charges attached to both of them, although the PM has managed to bluff his way through with plenty of denials."

"The charges will last all of maybe a year," said Bigsy, "Then they will be back in the swamp."

"Something about 'tea break's over, back on your heads!' " said Jake, "Oops! I just said out loud what I was thinking, again."

He paused, then said, "I learned to never buy a cloned electric vehicle, and to check for fire retardants!"

Lottie added, "And being around Clare never creates a dull moment."

"Although it can be dangerous," added Hannah.

"Cheers, everybody," said Clare. They chinked their 150th Cuvée Claret wine glasses together.

Sleaze

Ed Adams

Sleaze

Ed Adams

www.ingramcontent.com/pod-product-compliance
Lightning Source LLC
Chambersburg PA
CBHW062106040426
42336CB00042B/2258